Comme
LORD, MAKE US ONE

'Joel's thrilling and very readable
racial, social and theological ga
not compromising the gospel, \
with the satisfying feeling that the EA is in good hands.

Dr R T Kendall
Minister, Westminster Chapel

'He is brilliant, excited and an evangelical! I love stories and this one
is worth telling.'

Gerald Coates
Pioneer Church Leader

'Joel Edwards is one of the outstanding bridge builders of our time. He
has an unusual ability to bring together people who would otherwise
be divided by creed and conviction. That is the essence of Christian
living.'

Revd Matthew Ashimolowo
Pastor, Kingsway International Christian Centre

'In this warm and compelling human story, the author has demonstrated
an unerring facility for charting a steady course through the shoals and
currents of our evangelical voyage in recent years. For his fire, modesty
and wisdom, Joel Edwards can rightly be described in biblical terms as
"an ambassador of the churches and an honour to Christ".'

Revd Richard Bewes
Rector, All Souls Church

Lord, Make Us One – But Not All The Same!

Seeking Unity in Diversity

Joel Edwards

Hodder & Stoughton

LONDON SYDNEY AUCKLAND

British Library Cataloguing in Publication Data
A record for this book is available from the British Library

ISBN 0 340 72171 5

Typeset by Avon Dataset Ltd, Bidford-on-Avon, Warks
Printed and bound in Great Britain by
Clays Ltd St Ives Plc, Bungay, Suffolk

Hodder and Stoughton
A division of Hodder Headline Plc
338 Euston Road
London NW1 3BH

I would like to dedicate this book to those closest to me who graciously endured private readings of the raw material. To my wife Carol, who spurred me on against the odds and to our two children, Joel Junior and Davina, who gave me time off from being a father in order to share myself with others through this book.

Contents

Acknowledgments

This book has been an account of my own experience in diversity. To that extent I owe a great deal to many individuals who have inspired and walked with me over the years.

My thanks to Philip Mohabir, who was instrumental in my entry into contemporary evangelicalism and to my predecessor, Clive Calver, who has inspired so many of us to appreciate our different Christian traditions.

Special thanks to Mia and David Hilborn who read the manuscript and gave me the benefit of their insights, and to my administrative assistant, Diane Toothill, who went way beyond the call of duty in typing it up.

Finally, I am indebted to Catherine Butcher for editing the text with great skill and sensitivity, and for making many helpful comments.

I hope at the very least that the book will provoke some interesting thought and discussion!

Joel Edwards
November 1998

The Longest Day

The suggestion of sunshine greeted me as I stepped from the British Overseas Airways Corporation flight on to the tarmac at Heathrow. I was eight and it was May 1960. It was the end of a long transatlantic flight – my very first time outside Jamaica. But it was also the start of another journey. It had been a traumatic trip beginning with the awareness that I was to be wrenched away from the security of all that I had known for eight years. Friends, school, familiar sights and sounds were all to be exchanged for the fairy-tale reality of a place I only really knew about through nursery-rhyme history and Christmas card images. I cried all the way to the Palisaidos Airport in Kingston and my sorrow could hardly be contained. Neither my uncle's assurances that friends were easy to come by, nor the promise of a ride in his leather-seated Hillman Minx – not even the new sailor suit – helped very much.

The plane was full of awe-struck Jamaicans, most of whom had never previously left the island. They were being soothed and pampered by the professional smiles of White women, uniformly dressed. It was a strange sight as I settled into my seat between my two sisters. The unbridled panic of an adult passenger convinced that the plane was on fire as the propellers of the great bus fired up to taxi away was not particularly helpful. It was good to hear the nice White lady explaining through her smile that it was only smoke from the engine, and that it always happened when the engine was warming up.

As it turned out, the journey itself was the beginning of culture shock: an odd mixture of apprehension and adventure. It was as though all my senses were thrown into a violent process of reorientation. This was my introduction to tasteless food – I had never eaten food without seasoning before. The entire transatlantic experience became a process of cultural rebirth in the relentlessly humming womb of this great bus roaring above the clouds.

Numerous miniature memories of Jamaica migrated with my departure. The sound of laughter and carefree sun-filled days, odd moments of frightening fun by the beaches beyond Kingston, khaki school uniforms, the Union Jack and the quickly fading faces of friends. There was also the shadowy figure of my father hovering on the edge of my memories. I had few clear memories despite the fact that I spent eight years of my life with him. I had no recollection of words or any meaningful encounter. What I remembered of him could quickly be summarised: he was a carpenter who worked at a local college. He would arrive home each Friday evening carrying cheese in the saddle-bag of his bicycle. He was not kind to my mother. He was in fact a man in the house rather than a father in our home. He seemed to play no part in my recollections of leaving Jamaica. I could not remember hearing him say goodbye, although I imagine that he must have acknowledged the fact that three of his children were leaving for good.

But among all these childhood recollections were the abiding memories of my experience of New Town Church and the powerful charismatic figure of the pastor, Elder Shaw. Like a micro-chip embedded in the brain too delicate for safe retrieval, so this image of passionate preaching locked itself into my child-consciousness. Elder Shaw launched himself so completely into his preaching that, although I had no idea what he was talking about, it felt real, rather than just theory. Years later, when I read Equiano's description of his first impression of George Whitefield, I immediately thought of Elder Shaw. Olaudah Equiano, an ex-slave turned celebrity-journalist, saw Whitefield preaching to a packed house in Philadelphia and was struck by his energy and the fact that he was 'sweating as much as I ever did while in slavery on Montserrat beach'. In fact Equiano wondered why this kind of enthusiasm was so unusual in the clergy. Having heard Whitefield he concluded that he was 'no longer at a loss to account for the thin congregations they preached to'. It was this energy which I experienced as a small child and which left me with the most abiding memories of believable preaching. Apart from that, he always kept me awake in church.

There was too, an energy in the congregation which seemed to flow from the preaching style. Whatever the real size of the congregation, my impression was of a large crowd of worshippers, vibrant and vigorously creative, teeming with happy young men playing instruments. I could not remember any of them talking to me and I did not remember their names, but I admired them.

It never ceases to amaze me how much capacity for change is programmed into the human spirit. You can see it often in children and it was certainly true of my own journey from one cultural reality to another. I had stopped crying long before I arrived at Heathrow. Walking from the steps of the plane to the tarmac, my conscious thoughts were already moving forward.

I was just able to recognise my mother. She too struggled to come to terms with how thin I looked for my age. I was too distracted to register the full emotional impact of our arrival but I was aware that this was a poignant reunion.

There in the arrivals lounge the unspeakably bewildering void of two years was being filled in. It was hard for a six-year-old to understand the sudden disappearance of his mother. And yet it wasn't. I held in my small mind numerous memories of my mother's ordeals at the hands of my father. I relived the horrors of her helpless wailing and my silent pledges to put an end to it when I was old enough to do so. But before I was able to work out how old that would be, I woke one Monday morning to find that she was gone. It was strangely understandable. Years later I was to learn how she had skilfully planned her departure over many months, buying and storing clothes at my uncle's house and borrowing the money for her plane ticket. It was a careful operation designed to escape my father's detection and meticulously kept away from us as children. On that final Sunday she left the house to attend church for the last time. The only difference was that on this occasion she took my eldest sister part of the way, giving her instructions and committing her to secrecy. My mother left for England early the following morning.

The letters and Christmas cards had kept us in touch, but how was an eight-year-old to be prepared for such a reunion? I still cannot recall any specific words among the tears and hugs as we reached across the lost months to rediscover each other and as I gazed at the faces of relatives and friends I had never met. There in the arrivals lounge at Heathrow in London, England, we were reshaping our future.

It seemed a long car ride to Kentish Town in north-west London. We pulled into Haverstock Road and my uncle told us that we were almost there. A few moments later we pulled up at a front door. I was shocked and deeply disappointed. In Jamaica we had our own house in its own yard. Here, it seemed, I was being brought to live in a factory! It had to be a factory. I had seen Dickensian drawings in my books at school and I knew that all homes in England were quaint snow-capped cottages – usually with a robin red-breast perched on the gate post. At least, that's what the Christmas cards showed and no one had told me differently. Terraced properties were definitely a foreign concept.

It was my longest day. But this was my new reality. I was in England with my two sisters and mother. I had come to the mother country I had heard so much about and for which I was nurtured in unquestioned patriotism. In our school we were watched over by the Union Jack from its permanent position in the corner of the classroom, a symbol of the Commonwealth. By the time I left Jamaica I knew by heart the words of 'I Vow to Thee, My Country' sung to Holst's Jupiter movement in *The Planets* suite.

School life in Britain was the consolidation of culture shock. I was shocked by the idea of free school milk under the health care provisions. Fish and chips in newspapers, baked beans and 'half loaves' of sliced bread at the corner shop were all culture shocks. I was always different and without trying to, everyone in school reminded me of my difference. For reasons I could not fully understand school lessons suddenly became more difficult: it felt almost as though the rules about learning had changed. Children can be brutal without realising the depth of their hostilities. I quickly learned that I was different. There were only a handful of Black children in Carlton Primary School in Kentish Town. I soon became an object of curiosity and intrigue: the recently arrived pupil with the strange accent and woolly hair everyone wanted to touch. In Jamaica I was like everyone else; the idea of being different never occurred to me. Now I had become a 'coloured boy' in the classroom. Relationships were also very strange. I had two close friends in primary school both of whom remained friends into secondary education. One was another Black pupil named Errol Rowe, the other an English boy, Martin

Hollingsworth. It always seemed strange that I had free access to Errol's house and he would often visit my home, while Martin, on the other hand, seldom came to my house and I was never allowed past his front door.

The explosion of cultural discovery continued throughout my primary school experience; understanding what education was all about seemed very secondary. In fact, it seemed as though I grew through my primary school experience by remote control and without any conscious input beyond the classroom.

My mother did two or sometimes three menial jobs to keep things going in the home. All of her energy was taken up with work and church attendance. She had no idea how the education system worked nor any time to find out, as economic survival rightly took priority. She drove herself to earn enough to pay the air fares for five children and a grandson within a short period of time, as well as maintaining a single-parent household.

I knew that it wasn't just me, because my two sisters were also finding things difficult, although in a different way. I overheard conversations about demotivation and boredom in their secondary school experience, and frustrated complaints about doing lessons they had already completed in Jamaica.

I failed my Eleven Plus. I had no idea what it was about or its long-term significance. Secondary school in Summer's Town near Mornington Crescent was a curious cocktail of continued cultural transition and the beginning of academic pursuits. Sir William Collins was a large comprehensive in a rough area which also aspired to a reasonable standard of excellence. I was a member of a single-parent household. By this time I shared my domestic life with all four older sisters, a nephew who was only a year and a half younger than me and a number of other members of our extended family.

In socio-economic terms we were a poor family. 'Poor' meant free school meals and uniforms. I still recall the stigma of the free dinner line and the pains I went to in timing it so that I could collect my dinner ticket without having to queue. It was an art form which had become particularly difficult by the time I was elected house captain in my fifth year and, two years later, became the first Black school captain in the school's history. There was something vaguely incongruous about a head boy on free school meals who occasionally represented the school at the local Rotary Club and met distinguished visitors on the headmaster's behalf.

Secondary school was also about the challenge of living out my faith in a hostile environment. There were times when I struggled to balance my role as the head boy of a large school which barely acknowledged Christianity with my own deep commitment to Christ, which was well known to the staff and most of the pupils. I began to learn, in that task, that people do not have to agree with you to value you. It seemed so often that my greatest asset was a growing capacity to value and respect others with whom I disagreed and who were unable to understand what I was all about as a Christian. Respect appeared to be the key. I kept getting the impression that most pupils trusted me – even when I crept up on them at the back of the playground and confiscated their gambling prize, or pointed them in the headmaster's direction for their misdemeanours. Staff gave me the impression that I was a safe pair of hands, although few agreed with my faith.

I'm sure that I met racism during my time at school but it wasn't an issue in the mid to late 1960s. It was seldom blatant: only one occasion springs to mind, when a self-important boy offered me a fight in the playground. Mostly, it was rather subtle evidences of marginalisation which appeared from time to time: odd comments with an ugly angle or the attitude which suggested that I was unlikely to do as well as I wished to do. I still recall the shock waves which went through the school when a sixth form student gained a place in Oxford. His name was Laddie Salanke and he was an African.

My journey from my arrival in 1960 to my closing months of schooling was a precarious path along the way to identity. I was part of a growing band of the Caribbean diaspora who lived in two worlds: a Black person at home but someone with a different cultural persona once the front door closed behind me. It was the unconscious development of a cultural dualism which became the norm for many in those early days of immigration. I was an outsider. I knew that I was from Jamaica but was no longer sure whether I was Jamaican or British: I had two passports. My experiences of school made it abundantly clear that I was not really like most of my fellow pupils and I often felt that I was inhabiting two worlds, one in which I existed without effort and the wider world of school and society in which my existence and sense of belonging came only with conscious effort.

It became increasingly clear to me that my greatest stability and clearest point of reference was my faith in God: the inner voice of unspecified vocation and the powerful affirmation which came with the experience of worshipping in a community of faith where my own identity was effortlessly affirmed and sustained. It was what social analysts and historic church leaders began to describe as the Black Church.

2

First Steps

The trek from home to church always seemed such a long way. On reflection it was probably due to the fact that it was several miles, and from our home in Kentish Town to the small Scout hall in Kensal Rise, north-west London, was an interminable journey for an eight-year-old. I was mildly bemused by the fact that we passed so many other churches on the way. Members converged on the hall from various points across London. For all I know, this kind of activity in the 1960s could have been one of the earlier examples of the 'gathered church' which has become much more common in cosmopolitan settings.

Usually we had to clear up before we got down to worship. It often meant sweeping out the discarded cigarette ends and sometimes the odd can, and setting the chairs out. Worship was spontaneous. In time I grew to recognise that it had its own essential unwritten liturgy. To an outsider the worship service could easily appear to have no order as it seemed to unfold spontaneously over three or four hours. In fact there were fairly precise expectations about how things were done and, while there were also times when 'the Spirit took over', generally what we had was a kind of organised spontaneity. There were fixed points of reference. Most services began with 'singspiration' – what might now be called the worship – then prayer and a Bible reading.

Invariably, this would be followed by a series of personal testimonies, solos or other individual contributions; tithes and offerings were gathered; then, finally, came the sermon. Sermons seldom concluded without a strong appeal for response, either for personal conversion, healing or some other specific encounter with God. Across the Black church scene you would rarely find an alternative pattern: most services were variations on the same themes.

Sermons usually exceeded an hour. Length seemed at times to be the qualifying element. But good preaching was story-telling at its best. Black churches did not tolerate lectures on Sundays and were deeply suspicious of preachers who relied on notes. Effective preaching was the ability to explore the biblical stories in such a way that the listener was brought into the presence of God. It could provoke unbearable fear about the terror of God or embrace the human spirit with unspeakable joy. Even as a child I was often afraid of the preacher, but curiously it wasn't the kind of fear which made me want to stay away the following week. It seemed to be a cleansing kind of fear. And, even as a child, I knew what it was to be so aware of the presence of God that it made me fearless on Monday mornings. Preachers always seemed to expect a human response to the presentation of the Gospel story. And they always spoke about 'signs following' the Word.

Not all preachers were equal to the task and an uninspired monologue was always an invitation to fidget. But the music helped. It is no accident that Black churches have turned out so many gifted musicians over the years. Worship is the vocabulary of the soul. It manages to include everyone in the conversation and draws whole communities together. Its pulling power was an essential feature of our church life. In that environment you chose to be excluded, but even tapping your feet meant you belonged. Worship brought us all together in a cacophony of praise: young and old, guitars, tambourines, hand-clapping and unrestrained screams of joy. It was not New Town Church in Kingston, but it offered me the security of the familiar. Here in this haven I breathed a natural air. It was natural and normal.

There at the dawn of my experience of church life in Britain I had no way of knowing the extent to which this oasis provided a life-line to so many from the Caribbean diaspora: the mums and dads in their mid twenties and thirties who had migrated as pioneers to Britain, leaving roots and relatives in pursuit of a better life in the mother country. They were patriots in the land of their spiritual parents, but it seemed ill prepared to receive them. They left an environment where over 69 per cent of the population went to church on Sundays and, defying the warnings about Britain's spiritual barrenness, they arrived to the chilly welcome of a post-Christian Britain where worshippers and churches were sometimes cold and unfriendly. Many things contributed to the importance of Sunday worship in the Black churches. On Sundays and during the mid-week prayer meetings they experienced the rejuvenation of their spirits and recovered a sense of worth which was so often suffocated in the course of the working week. Models of leadership, imperfect though they were, emerged from the congregation. In the Black church community, the icons occupied the pulpits and were distinguished by a leadership chemistry and an ability to move the listener as they perspired their way through the sermon. No one spoke of the 'priesthood of all believers' but anyone could pray and everyone was qualified to say something from the Bible. Few were perfect orators but everyone was encouraged to bring their gifts of worship to the gathering of the saints. Women and children were welcomed – even if they could not take a lead in giving the sacraments.

There was also the luxury of a certainty which came with a simplicity of faith. 'God said it and we believe it' was the credo of our uncomplicated faith in our God who brought us from the Caribbean. We loved the Bible and the Bible was for believing. Indeed, a simple worshipper armed with the Word was to be believed above a bishop or theologian without it. This was no random selection of personalised creeds but the corpus of faith and practice which held our uncompromising community together.

And our faith *was* uncompromising. We believed in the verbal inspiration of the Bible; that Jesus was born of the Virgin, the only begotten Son of God; that He lived, was crucified, raised on the third day, ascended and seated at the right hand of God. That the pre-millennial Second Coming would bring in a new kingdom, and finally He would judge the living and the dead. The righteous would go to heaven and the wicked to eternal damnation. These were things we did not always understand but we certainly believed them. We were evangelical without knowing it. It was uncomplicated, real faith backed up by real evidence: healing, personal experiences of answered prayers and ecstatic expressions of praise. Forgiveness and freedom. We spoke in tongues and cried if we wanted to. God seemed unperturbed by our emotions.

But belief was married to behaviour. Our Practical Resolutions went alongside our Basis of Faith. Even when the occasional case broke the surface of the disciplinary meeting we all knew that adultery, fornication and the like were definitely no-go areas. In those early days of the 1960s and 1970s, there was little merit in discussing the finer points of homosexuality, gambling, cinema-going or casual relationships. In fact, 'going out' was an uncomfortable phrase. Women wore hats and did not wear trousers. Men wore ties and did not wear beards. No one wore jewellery unless, of course, you were a visiting preacher or party from the United States, where it seemed that a somewhat lower standard of attire was permissible. It was generally known that 'nominal Christians' – Anglicans, Baptists and the like – fell outside the remit of credible Christianity, and to mingle too closely was generally inadvisable except for evangelism.

And evangelism was important. Everyone knew that God had sent us to the kingdom 'for such a time as this'. We were sufficiently different to be convinced that ideally everyone else should be as much like us as possible. Not only should they believe as we did, but if at all possible they should worship and look as we did. It was not easy to accommodate diversity. To be different was almost certainly to be deviant. To be deviant was to be disciplined.

Here, as far as we knew, was truth on fire. In reality a powerfully strange mix of cultures was compressed into our small Scout hall. Our latent African-ness mingled with the traits of an imbibed North American Pentecostalism which expressed itself as Caribbeans at worship. In this environment I was held upright to take my first steps as a young Christian. Even as a child, it was quite easy for me to fall into the language of a 'born-again' experience. It wasn't just that it was the lingua franca of my Christian environment, but simply that there was not a better description of what happened to me when I was eleven years old.

The London to Birmingham run for the Annual National Convention of the New Testament Church of God was a major expedition in the days before the M1 motorway. I have vague memories of a large exuberant gathering filled with towering adults whose major pre-occupation, apart from worshipping, was to stop children like me having a good time. Looking back through the telescope of years it seems as though my main preoccupa-tion was to salvage as much fun as possible from a regime of adult prohibitions.

At some point in the proceedings I met up with Bunny. I cannot remember where he came from and I suspect

Bunny was not his real name. We had a great time until our paths separated at the altar. It is still a great mystery to me why children gravitate towards the front pews where their ploys are more easily detected, but in any event that's where we were. The preacher finished his monologue. He may have been very good that day but I have no recollection of the sermon. It certainly was not one of the fearful ones; I was keenly tuned to those. The inevitable appeal for salvation followed the sermon and Bunny thought it would be fun to make a fallacious response.

'Last one to the altar is a monkey,' he challenged.

I did not want to be a monkey. 'Last one to the altar is a monkey,' I repeated. We agreed on the count of three.

'One, two, three!' I made a blind dash to the altar rail, but soon became conscious that Bunny was not near by. I peeked to my left and then to my right before glancing over my shoulder. I saw Bunny doubled up laughing. Evidently, he was happy to be a monkey. My first inclination was to get up, but just then I saw my mother beyond Bunny's heaving shoulder. She looked very pleased so I decided to stay. I closed my eyes on my calamity and on Bunny. As it transpired, I also closed my eyes on my past. It is not easy to describe what happened next except to say that I was overwhelmed by the most un-worldly recognition of guilt and forgiveness and wept uncontrollably for what seemed like a lifetime. I have never been able to get my mind around the phenomenon of a child, sheltered from the worst excesses of sinfulness as I was, feeling so guilty and then so forgiven. I was, in C.S. Lewis's words, 'surprised by joy'.

It seemed to be what adults called 'powerful' and it made me feel clean inside. It was strange and I knew that I didn't make it happen. Although I had been a church boy all my life, this was the beginning of a conscious commitment to follow Christ. I have never found a better description than being 'born again'. I never saw Bunny again but he had been very helpful to me.

My journey of a lifetime began consciously with that first step. And at what point, I wonder, does a journey become a pilgrimage? I still remember walking out of that church building wondering exactly what had happened and what I was to make of the happening.

Those early steps led to a series of encounters with God and discoveries about myself which lasted through the confusing episodes of teenage years and gave me a gentle introduction to aspects of public ministry which seemed to pursue me relentlessly. In many ways I was very lonely. Most of my friends had left school by the time I had reached the sixth form. I had good friends in the local church but I was never certain how many of them really understood the quiet driving force behind me. Through many failings and personal frustrations in my teenage years, the common feature was an insatiable passion for God. Nothing mattered quite as much. It was not a chore to make a double bus ride across London to join a handful of adults for the mid-week prayer meeting, even in winter. It was not remotely virtuous: a thirsty person does not calculate his options.

Strange private encounters took place during those desert years. Like the elderly English woman who turned up at our church one Sunday, spoke to me of her personal convictions about what God was saying to me, and then vanished into the night without speaking to another soul.

Eventually, not even quietly affirming encounters helped much. Things came to a critical point when I was nineteen. I walked to church on a sunlit day in May with my mind shrouded by clouds of desperation. A strange combination of loneliness and hunger for God resulted in intense spiritual and emotional distress. 'If you don't help me soon,' I prayed, 'I am through.' It wasn't meant to be a threat and I suspect God treated it in the spirit in which it was intended:

the groaning of a desperate teenager.

That night the church service was amazing. I stood rigid in a sea of animated worshippers. Children who barely had any notions of biblical truths, such as I possessed, joined seasoned Christians in swirling torrents of dance and effortless praise. It all seemed so unfair. But before I had a chance to complain I was overtaken by superlative and unfiltered love. It had nothing to do with anything around me. It was as if my capacity to love filled the universe. And with it came boundless joy. This joy owed nothing to other people's enjoyment of God. And then from inside my mind or spirit rushed a vocabulary which I did not initiate. It seemed to be a language from beyond my own powers of comprehension, but which did not violate my intellect. With my mind fully intact I heard myself speaking a language I did not understand and which no one had taught me. I had heard it described for years and had often seen others doing it. My behaviour was not normal but I was not ashamed. We called it 'speaking in tongues' and it was in the Bible and our official Minutes Book.

Even so I didn't fully understand it, but I wished it would never end. This rushing stream of joy seemed to fill up the spiritual hunger and thirst of my teenage years. I have often thought about that moment and its bewildering reality. What happened to me was far too powerful to have been mere emotionalism. What was being poured into my teen-age life was a quality of joy and love which completely overwhelmed me. I could only imagine that that kind of love must be what God Himself is like.

This dramatic experience of God was a significant watershed in a number of ways. It was the culmination of a personal quest for an experience which I had longed for. To be 'filled with the Spirit' was the hallmark of authentic Pentecostalism. Its expressions were all around me from childhood days. The ability to speak in tongues was the evidence of baptism in the Holy Spirit, a prerequisite, not only to certain areas of ministry, but often as an emblem of true spirituality. Unfortunately it often seemed that there was no doubt about it: the baptism was the line of demarcation between second- and first-class Christians. No one ever said this in so many words. It was for me, though, the psychological summary after many years of an emphasis on this phenomenon. It infused the preaching culture, and everyone aspired to it as it earned credit points in the monthly church reports and often determined your eligibility for ministry.

In my early years I heard numerous sermons which equated this experience with the oil in the wise virgins' lamps which made them ready for the Bridegroom. To put it another way: the same things which made you unable to receive 'the Blessing' were likely to make you unprepared for the Second Coming of Christ. Ironically, the very things which were aimed at bringing us closer to faith in God alienated me from His presence, reducing me to a nervous insecurity. Instead of the wonder of sonship, I had often been plagued with feelings of estrangement and crushing inferiority. My focus on my personal failings displaced loving faith in God. Invariably, my own private census of the mini-bus or the small prayer meeting would reveal the fact that I was the only one without 'the Blessing'. So spiritually insecure had I become that my inner being had grown uneasy about the presence of God. I wanted God more than anything else and yet remained afraid of His presence. In a sense He had sneaked up on me from behind during this worship service in my local church. Now, after I had wept my way around numerous venues in a nervous search for God, here, in my own local church, at a time I least expected it, God sneaked up on me from behind, as it were, to surprise me with His joy. I suspect He knew what I would have done if I had seen Him coming first.

But it was a watershed. There on that evening I joined the ranks of those who had 'arrived'. I had crossed the sound barrier and spoken in tongues. The gateway to greater activity would be opened to me. But it soon became far more meaningful than that. It was very evident to me that there was something quite powerful about this pheno- menon. A few weeks later, shortly before my twentieth birthday, I was asked to speak on the return of Christ. I was not the only one who noticed the difference in my delivery. It was not a detailed or particularly thought-through presentation of the pre-millennial position according to our own theological brand. But it was a noticeably fluent and passionate word of encouragement and challenge about present lifestyle, based on the reality of Christ's coming. Most of us were surprised. Several people were moved to tears.

It was not long afterwards that I preached for the first time in our national youth camp. One night I had been greatly impressed to scribble a few thoughts on a theme, 'God's Relay System'. It was a challenge to young people to consider themselves suitable for ministry and to recognise that God uses young people in perpetuating the witness of the Gospel. The very next day I was asked to speak during the evening. My brief address was followed by one of the most incredible sights I had ever seen to that point. The evening meeting became an explosion of unusual personal encounters with God, with large numbers of young people making serious commitments to Him.

In day-to-day life, after three years in the sixth form, I left with three A levels and began my first experience of the 'real' world of work. It was an important in-between time. I gave up my part-time job filling shelves in Tesco and spent just over a year as a junior clerk at the Kentish Town head office of Dunn and Co., the men's clothing company. My introduction to 'full-time' work was a gentle treadmill period of orientation to the adult world of work. The tediously repetitive tasks were only made bearable by the novelty of 'full-time' wages.

In spite of these new experiences there were very clear inner signals pushing me in a new direction and suggesting that I had not arrived. I was only continuing an important pilgrimage with God. It was not long after that I felt I was being nudged in a new direction. A hunger for the Bible pushed me beyond the otherwise adequate provisions of my home church in Willesden, which had been my spiritual home. In fact it would be better to say that the powerful presentation of our pastor's preaching stimulated a greater desire for the Bible. It so happened that my plans to study sociology did not work out, and with A levels to my credit I was being encouraged to enrol in one of our denominational Bible colleges in America or Europe. They were a long way from home. But Rudolph Kennedy, my local pastor and spiritual mentor, made a new discovery. He came across a 'good college' in a far-flung corner of Middlesex, south of Watford in an area called Northwood, which was just starting a new BA Theology degree. Northwood – wherever that was – seemed a strange place to have a college called London Bible College but the prospectus looked good. In any event, on the map it was a lot nearer than America or Germany.

3

Crossing Over

I had no idea what was in store for me as I approached the driveway to Aldis House in London Bible College. The previous three months had flown by in a haze of activity as I went through the process of application and interview. Within a short period of time I had found myself ambling up the driveway of the college campus tucked away off Green Lane in Northwood. It was much smaller than I anticipated, and I had to adjust to the community feel of the place as opposed to the rambling impersonal campus I had imagined because of my Easter weekends at Leicester University during our national youth conventions.

This was to be my first ever interview. It was a mutual discovery exercise between me and the interviewing faculty. I was struck by the graciousness with which the interview was conducted, the sensitive prayer for guidance and the impression which persisted throughout that, as a Black Pentecostal, I would be something of a novelty.

'Not all students here will be comfortable with things like speaking in tongues,' my main interviewer pointed out. 'How would you deal with that?' Whatever I said must have been good, but it was clear that the college had had few full-time students from my background before. I got the impression that they were taking a calculated risk, while I was taking a leap into the unknown. It was apparent that we spoke in different theological and cultural languages. I reckoned that I was as committed to the Bible as any other person in the room, but it must have been fairly evident that terms like 'an evangelical institution' and associated concepts were not ringing any bells with me. I recognised few of the personalities, evangelical trade marks or signals which emerged during the course of the interview, but I left with a clear impression that I would be allowed into this new and unfamiliar world.

With only three months to the start of term, life became a blur of preparation. Within a few days I was applying for a student grant and opening a bank account for the first time in my life. The advance reading list, which included Wenham's *The Elements of New Testament Greek*, added a sense of foreboding to the adventure and anticipation as the new academic year drew near.

A few days before my twenty-first birthday I returned to London Bible College in the sunshine of an October day to begin life as a theological student. I had no real idea what lay ahead of me as I approached the driveway to Aldis House on the edge of the site, but the next three years at this strange place were to become the crucible in which God would shape many things for the future.

I occupied a ground-floor room with two new students, David Brown and John Hards. I learned a great deal, for in those early months I came face to face with an important fact: God had a lot more children than I had been led to believe and a lot more friends than I knew about. Thankfully we had been well prepared for this shock of diversity by the wise, laid-back insights of the principal, Gilbert Kirby. During our orientation week, he told us that we were likely to encounter beliefs and convictions which differed significantly from our own. He also told us that it was more than likely that, in this interdenominational, international, evangelical academy, Baptists were likely to leave more

Baptist, Anglicans more Anglicans, and so on. I cannot remember if he mentioned anything about Pentecostals but his attitude was very inclusive.

He was right. Despite numerous heated theological debates, I cannot think of anyone who defected from their denomination as a result of their time at LBC.

During my first year, I was in intense culture shock. Well-known evangelical names and ideas, which I had never heard of, exploded in my mind throwing me into information overload. What was common evangelical chat for many of my fellow students became an assault of the unfamiliar. Added to that, I had to adjust to the fact that people who were very unlike me seemed genuinely converted. Actually it was worse: some of them appeared to have as much love for the Bible and Christ as I did. Some had even given up good jobs to study the Bible and had committed themselves to mission in ways which I had not contemplated. Others, who had never shown any signs of my own Pentecostal fervour, evidently had a clear grasp of the mind of the Spirit in the Church and the world. Those three years, between 1972 and 1975, were the crucial formative years of my pilgrimage.

But one of my greatest lessons was not theological: I discovered that I was definitely not an Englishman. In my previous world, before this cultural unveiling at LBC, it had been natural to live between cultures. Having learned the art of cultural adaptation, it was easy to assume that I was actually the same as the next man. My first year in a dormitory with two true Englishmen shook me into a new reality: I was a Black Britisher. It was only then that I came to realise the degree to which I, along with many other young men and women in pre-Black-consciousness Britain, ran the gauntlet between cultures in order to be understood in both. To live in the wider world of school and work I made an effortless psychological shift which subconsciously adapted to the English culture. In this world, thoughts, accent and even sense of humour went through a cultural recasting. Instinctively, I knew that Jamaican jokes would not translate well in the playground!

I was a product of a 1960s Britain in which a whole generation of Black children closed the front door behind them in the mornings to assume another identity, then reverted to an equally real but truer self at the end of the day. There was no conscious effort to play an English role, although we were always aware of an unspoken obligation to wear the costume in order to go with the flow. We had an uncanny ability to get back to the cultural nest and find unthinking refuge in what was truly natural. To return to the narrower familiarities of home and church, and recline in Caribbeanisms, was refreshing: the emotional equivalent of a warm soak at the end of an eventful day. At a stroke, all that was familiar was swept away at LBC. Gone was my route back to the haven of Blackness which had always been mine at the end of the school day or the weekend. There was no escape from Englishness: it was a twenty-four-hour culture. At LBC no one understood the importance of rice and peas with chicken on Sundays or knew what to do with a plantain!

The whole issue became particularly poignant when, in my second year, a good friend noticed that my very limited library included two books on Black history and declared in bewilderment, 'Will the real Joel Edwards please step forward!' Even though my friend saw it as no more than a passing remark, it was a defining moment for me. The real challenge was to discover others in this new world without losing myself, to build bridges from my experience to those around me in order to become enriched by others' understanding of the same God.

For the first time I found myself in a multicultural church community. I met White students from South Africa and found to my surprise that I had to deal with the discomfort evoked by the Afrikaner accent. I came across Black colleagues from Kenya, Zimbabwe, Ghana and Nigeria and was intrigued to find that they understood the culture of British evangelicalism better than I did. Through their own links with European missions, they had been enfranchised by the international language of evangelicalism, along with those from America and other parts of the world.

But this was also my first meeting with other Pentecostals from different denominations. I had heard about Pentecostals outside our doctrinal fences; the impression I had been given was that they were vaguely compromised for reasons I could not quantify – apart from the fact that they allowed jewellery and didn't seem to preach as hard as we did. The people from Elim believed, like us, in a centralised structure but the gulf of foot-washing remained between us: we did it whenever we had communion and they did not. The Assemblies of God were rather more distant. We were not quite sure what to do with a de-centralised Pentecostal organisation.

What was particularly bewildering was to find other Christians who believed in the work and sovereignty of the Holy Spirit as I did, but who were not as committed to the same apparently infallible truths I had come to rely on. They were, it seemed, less insistent on a pre-millennial understanding of Christ's return: that Jesus would rule on the earth for a thousand years before the final judgment and the beginning of eternal bliss. Equally alarming was the fact that some of them did not believe that speaking in tongues was the *initial evidence* of the baptism of the Holy Spirit. There was undoubtedly a more laid-back approach to worship which lacked the intensity with which I was so familiar. Very little around me reflected the same kind of separated 'holiness' ethos which had become the hallmark of my own Christian culture. On the whole, people seemed to be busy getting on with what they were doing rather than defining what they should not be doing.

I also knew I was crossing a new frontier when a fellow student mentioned the name of Martyn Lloyd-Jones in a casual conversation. When I asked who he was, I could see the incredulity on my colleague's face: 'You don't know who Martyn Lloyd-Jones is?' he asked. I felt like someone about to be disqualified from an important event as I explained sheepishly that I had never heard the name before. I could see how shocked he was and later came to understand why. But then, I had never heard of John Stott, Francis Schaeffer, James Packer or David Watson. Evangelical household names were total strangers to me. I kept discovering that their thoughts and writings had filtered down to me but I had never heard their names. My young world view had been shaped entirely by our own international leaders, like Ray Hughes, and leading figures in modern Pentecostalism, such as A.A. Allen, T.L. Osborn, Morris Cerullo and the great Christian ambassador Dr Billy Graham. To be truthful, I was stunned that he was shocked by my ignorance, particularly as he had no idea about my heroes who had international ministries reaching out to many thousands across the world.

And I had never come across Calvinism before. Both Jacobus Arminius, the sixteenth-century protagonist of Arminianism, and John Calvin were new discoveries for me. But I had a head start on Arminianism as my own denomination had been very influenced by the holiness roots of Methodism and presented a very consistent Arminian position. For the first time I met people who described themselves as 'Reformed' evangelicals. I deeply admired the precise tidiness of their position as I came to understand the issues, although I was often left with the impression that they did not quite know what to do with some of the experiences I brought to the discussions.

In this setting I was not confronted with abstract ideas about God, but with fellow evangelicals who came to these important questions from different biblical perspectives. I was presented with ideas I had never heard about and points of view which made me uncomfortable. The foundations of my own position remained secure but the walls were irrevocably shaken. It appeared that for the first time in my life I came to discover that it was not good enough to believe what you were asked to believe, but that you needed a reason for doing so. What also began to emerge was that the platform of biblical truth was far wider and stronger than I had appreciated before.

As the three years unfolded, many of us experienced important paradigm shifts in our thinking and attitudes. It became evident that true biblical holiness was something larger than organisational preferences and private prejudices. From our different positions we were held together by certain essential features of faith and commitment, to which we all held. That the Bible is God's Word to us; that Jesus is uniquely the Son of God, sharing the same essential nature with God the Father and the Holy Spirit; that Jesus' birth, life, ministry, death and resurrection were all truly miraculous and yet to be believed; that He left the earth to return in final triumph over evil and death itself; that the Church, meanwhile, has been given a commission to spread the good news of the Bible which says that forgiveness and hope for humankind comes only through life in the resurrected Christ by the power of the Holy Spirit. These seemed to be non-negotiable points of faith around which an international group of students from a range of Christian organisations and experiences met without much compromise or controversy. Beyond that, the classroom and casual encounters left room for a good deal of diversity and animated debate as well as serious disagreements. There were also significant debates about the modes of biblical inspiration, the Reformers' understanding of the elements in the Lord's Supper, the Second Coming and the use of spiritual gifts in the Church.

Prior to my time at LBC my understanding was that there was only one authentic way to worship: the Black Pentecostal way. It wasn't that anyone actually said this. It was just that all kinds of subliminal messages had been implanted over the years. For one thing there was the notion around that the reference in 1 Timothy 3:15 to the Church of the living God as the 'pillar and ground of the truth' was an oblique reference to our own denomination, the New Testament Church of God, rather than any reference to the universal Church. The claim was never made openly but it was only too easy to assume, given the fact that we were rather insular and a little uneasy with any other forms of worship. Even our own historic cousins – the Church of God of Prophecy – were kept at arm's length. There seemed little doubt that we had the authorised version of biblical Christianity and other groups had pale reflections of the true thing. We never believed that we were perfect. Like all other church communities we had our fair share of shortcomings and mistakes. But our attitudes to Scripture, ethics and worship were all held together by a comprehensive conviction: we were fairly certain that we were right.

In the spirit of true evangelicalism, we had a high view of Scripture and a holy hostility against all forms of criticism which sought to undermine its authority. Invariably, this defence of Scripture led to suspicion of the kind of nominalism which was often bred by academic professionalism. But it also meant an attitude to Scripture which put a higher value on books such as Joel, the Gospels, Acts and Revelation, which resonated with our own experience of God. The whole Bible was taken seriously: it was just that *some parts* were taken more seriously. All parts were inspired but we did find some parts more inspiring.

In the New Testament Church of God it was important to adhere to the pre-millennial Second Coming of Christ, to sanctification as a second and distinct work of grace, to speaking in tongues as the initial evidence of the baptism of the Holy Spirit, not only as a Pentecostal distinctive, but as a mark of Christian commitment; to believe less than this was to be a nominal Christian.

Our view of Scripture, together with a very strong emphasis on the imminent return of Christ, meant that we had a particularly high ethical code. It's probably also true to say that the Caribbean church culture fought for many years to undo the legacy of slavery which undermined fidelity in family life. Added to that, we were also the product of a strong culture of prohibition carried over from our long-standing links with Southern States Pentecostalism. Like other Christian groups I was later to learn about, Black Pentecostalism insisted that sexual practices outside marriage were totally outlawed. Homosexuality was not a matter for discussion. Similarly, casual relationships between members of the opposite sex were generally frowned upon so that to talk about having a 'girlfriend' or a 'boyfriend' was beyond our normal vocabulary. Relationships were understood only within the context of engagement for a limited period before marriage. We were not allowed to smoke, attend cinemas or theatres, use make-up or wear jewellery. It was forbidden to drink any liquor or strong drink – although no one seemed to mind it in wedding and birthday cakes.

All of these distinctive features were sustained in the context of fellowship and worship. This was the place where our values were quietly policed and reinforced. Consequently, organisational familiarity and authentic truth became inseparable. The worship experience was therefore the forum in which orthodoxy was monitored and against which others would be assessed. Those who did not appear to be like us were either pitied or targeted, though sometimes they were secretly admired.

In sharp contrast to my experience of worship at my home church, worship in the LBC chapel was like a cold shower in autumn. Everything seemed controlled and ordered. It did not seem to be advisable to raise hands in praise, except on rare occasions. No one shouted. Unfamiliar hymns appeared and no chorus was ever sung more than twice! In this setting, the terms of reference had changed and demanded a new lexicon in order to make sense of the experience. My new surroundings forced me to face a God who could still be active in the stayed silence of a conservative environment with a quality of worship which was not measured in decibels.

I noticed too, as I moved beyond the confines of the college setting, that much of the Christian world beyond my own was a lot quieter. To hear God would require a kind of spiritual and theological redialling. That was certainly my experience during my first visit to a large Pentecostal service in Watford during my first year as a student. It was evidently Pentecostal and louder than the college chapel. It was vibrant and full. The preaching was good, animated and engaging. But in a million ways I could not properly identify, it did not really feel Pentecostal. For a start, the pastor lacked the preaching stamina which I associated with proper Pentecostalism. They didn't have a choir and they did not clap properly.

The need for redialling was particularly brought home to me through two simple but memorable experiences. I first visited Goldhill Baptist Church under the instigation of a fellow student, Alistair Begg. I had never met the minister, Jim Graham, before, but watching from the balcony I was immediately struck by his profound pastoral gifting and generous spirit. His sermon was probably very good, but I have no recollection of it. What did strike me, and influenced me very deeply in my own pastoral work many years later, was the way in which he conducted a baby's dedication. It was the most natural and uncontrived dedication I had ever seen. It might just as well have been a father nestling his own infant in his own front room. I thought I recognised what we normally called 'a man of God' though he couldn't have been more different from the preaching 'icons' I was used to at home.

My second lesson came during a student placement at a sleepy, struggling Methodist church in Ruislip, Middlesex. A small group of us spent a year holding things together in the dwindling congregation. My first task was in co-ordinating the small Sunday School with a group of enthusiastic children from unchurched backgrounds. In some ways it felt like a simple step up from my experience of handling first-year pupils in the school playground. But I also became aware that these children were simply not the same as the nine- to eleven-year-old class I had worked with for years in my own church in Willesden, where the children had been brought up in church and were familiar with Christian language and concepts. The Methodist church in Ruislip also introduced me to the Methodist circuit system, which brought a variety of preachers, some of whom were less than evangelical in their convictions.

One Sunday a woman preacher came to speak and directed us to Romans chapter eight, which focuses on our security in Christ.

'Have you ever wondered how someone can be "more than a conqueror"?' she asked rhetorically. I had never thought to ask. 'A conqueror is someone who fights and wins,' she intoned. 'A "more than conqueror" is someone who fights and cannot lose.' Her sermon was both gracious and incisive, and probably did more than anything else to help me listen to preachers who did not raise their voice in the pulpit.

I heard excellent expositions from members of staff and skilled Bible teachers who came through the chapel from time to time. In those early days of my new-found pilgrimage I understood what was not naturally me, but also grew to learn that I could feed from the wider table God provided.

For the first time in my Christian experience I was a guest in a spiritual environment which was not my natural habitat. In spite of its international composition, the host culture was White anglo-evangelical. There was very little which effectively reflected my own background or a wider world view. But with students drawn from across the globe, each with their differences, I was no exception and that had distinct advantages. At no time did I feel that there was a cultural conspiracy to marginalise and it was far more preferable to be weaned in an environment which was closer to home than I would have been if I had gone to the United States to study in my denominational setting. A visit to old friends during my first year at LBC made it abundantly clear that they were on the dark side of the moon in comparison to my experience in England, even though they attended 'our own college' in the States. Then again, there was the distinct advantage of having my presuppositions challenged both by the faculty and by fellow students who saw things very differently.

By the end of my first year, I knew I was the richer for being where I was, even though I was equally aware that it was not without cost. I knew I would never be the same person. The problem was that others from my own church community also came to the same conclusion and were not entirely happy with the transition. I had left for college with a fanfare of good wishes, prayers and expectations. Many who had known me since early childhood had mapped out a course for me: I would study for three years, returning to take up a short-term appointment as a youth leader, before scaling the heights of the local pastorate en route to even greater things.

I suspect that few took me seriously when I announced at my farewell service that I had no long-term plans: that I simply felt that God was calling me to study and that this was just the next step on an unknown journey. During my first long summer holiday, it was obvious that I was going through some kind of spiritual shift which few people were prepared for. I was not living up to expectations. I did not always wear a tie on Sundays and it was becoming apparent that my mind was preoccupied with more questions than pre-selected answers. I now heard the criticisms of other churches with less tolerance and asked equally tough questions of ourselves.

Few people, either in college or within my church, understood the extent to which I wandered in no-man's-land as I chased between both worlds in pursuit of myself. The church which had been my familiar place and provided the crucible in which my identity had been forged now became remote. During the college terms, home life and church would vanish away as the earth recedes from the cockpit of a space capsule to reappear again as a welcome and familiar sight on return. The problem was that the re-entry invariably felt warm and rather bumpy. It would have been far easier had I decided to defect. But at heart I was the same person with the same convictions and theological preferences. I still had confidence in the substance of my faith and perspectives: it was just that I was no longer so convinced about some of the wrappings. Any astronaut would agree that the world will always be 'home' even though it may look very different from a distance.

The tensions diminished in my latter years in college as I found a happier medium. I had gained a lot in compensation from others and hoped that they also gained from my contributions. I had learned new concepts, had a better grasp of my Christian faith and felt that I had begun to know God better. But of equal importance was the fact that I had also grown to know many new people from around the world who had helped to stimulate and challenge my faith without destroying my identity. I had arrived a newcomer to the world of British evangelicalism with no clear notion of what I was to become beyond Bible college. I approached graduation aiming to take up training as a probation officer, but with no plans beyond that.

What I could never realise at that time was the degree to which God had sovereignly instigated friendships and networks that would last many years and which would later blossom into working relationships. God's investment in me was partly in the new things I had learned, but it had much more to do with the new people I had met. I came to realise how much other people help us make sense of God, His work and His Word. Truth can be comfortably constructed in erudite volumes but truth and grace are impossible without people. And God's classroom for me was not a solitary enclosure. It was, in fact, made up of fellow learners who were very unlike myself; it was a learning environment with which the twelve disciples themselves would empathise.

I find it hard to believe that so much happened in such a short time. Soon after my arrival, I had heard about Bob Horn, who became General Secretary of the University and Colleges Christian Fellowship; Lyndon Bowring, who went on to lead CARE (Christian Action Research and Education) and Clive Calver, my predecessor at the Evangelical Alliance. Their names were still reverberating off the college corridors. I was one of over fifty students on the college's new degree course with the Council for

National Academic Awards (CNAA). As it transpired I also had the privilege of studying with many contemporaries who have emerged to play prominent roles in current evangelicalism: people such as Ian Coffey, formerly EA's Field Team Director and currently Senior Pastor at Mutley Baptist in Plymouth; Steve Clifford, chairman of March for Jesus and a senior leader in the Pioneer network of New Churches; Ken Gnanakan from India, an international speaker and Director of In Contact Ministries; and Mary Evans, an author and member of the LBC faculty – to name but a few.

I had been introduced to a host of new names, taught by some of the finest teachers in British evangelicalism and had more books than I ever owned before. Incidentally, at LBC I learned to play table tennis and discovered peanut butter and jam sandwiches. I was a member of a Black and White music group called Zebra. I realised I was not cut out to be a wrestler after a friendly bout with a fellow student with one leg. And, along with three benign accomplices, I raided another Bible college in the early hours of the morning, removing their dinner gong as an act of just retribution. I came away with lots of good memories and, while others groaned about student poverty, I felt I had never had it so good. For the first time I had had my own bank account and a room all to myself.

But, after three short years, it was time to leave. Consumed by the intensity of final examinations, then awaiting results, the last few months included spasms of longing to get back to what we kept calling 'the real world'. Graduation came in the summer of 1975. I have little recollection of the content of the graduation service but it felt like a very important punctuation mark in my life. I had arrived at college with few firm plans for the future; by this time I had added a few more.

I knew it was likely that I would be getting married

34

within a year or so. Carol and I had known each other for four years, since before I started college. During my final year at LBC my occasional trips to Maidstone where she worked as a nurse had become a standing joke with those who knew me well. My thoughts about the Probation Service had developed further as I came towards the end of my student life. My only period of uncertainty about this came during a chapel service when a good friend leaned in my direction and asked if I really wanted to be a probation officer for the rest of my life.

Most of all I knew that I wanted to get back home – to the fourth-floor flat in north London which I shared with my mother and nephew. My mother, now in her sixties, had never really grown accustomed to my absence, although she had put on a good performance. And I wanted to get back to full participation in my local church.

There would be little point in pretending that I was exactly the same. The spectacles through which I formerly viewed the world now had new lenses: I would inevitably see things differently. I had learned to appreciate the diversity of God's work in people and now knew that to discover others need not mean losing my own identity. I had learned that compromise was not bad when it was appropriate, although it was sometimes very difficult to know when it was a good way forward rather than the easy way out. I knew that God didn't feel as uneasy about jewellery as I did and that, although a lot may be said for it, being a teetotaller did not necessarily offer a fast track to heaven. I understood that people did not automatically end up with a negative balance sheet with God simply because they spent an evening at the cinema. On the way to these conclusions I had found out that Augustine was a chauvinist who thought that spiritual gifts died out with the apostles; that Martin Luther was partial to a pint; that Wesley carried a flask of whisky in his inside cloak for the chilly nights and argued with George Whitefield about eternal salvation. And that Charles Haddon Spurgeon smoked a pipe. Even the revered Dr Billy Graham did not believe that speaking in tongues was the initial evidence of the baptism of the Holy Spirit. I did not know what to do with these characters. They did not fit my world view but they all transformed church history and everyone quoted them in their sermons.

London Bible College could not meet all my needs. We enjoyed each other's company and the college gave me a great deal, but did not really understand me. Now it was time to return home again. The umbilical cord had been stretched but never severed. My foundational convictions remained intact. Gilbert Kirby, the wise old man of evangelicalism, was right: I was as Pentecostal when I left as when I arrived. I still believed that there was a distinct overflowing work of the Spirit which happened in the life of a Christian apart from conversion, which manifested itself in unlearned languages and prophetic statements. That the gifts of the Spirit were still available to the believer for the good of the Church. And that there was a quality of life into which the community of faith may enter when it takes more seriously the sovereignty of the Holy Spirit who still has the right to free us from the shackles of our liturgical constraints from time to time. I still believed in the baptism of the Holy Spirit as it appears in Acts 2. And although I had learned and admired so much excellent exposition, I was still convinced that there was a genre of preaching which not only informed the mind and brought the Bible to clearer view, but which also brought the believer to God Himself. I had missed the radical call to the kind of holiness which pushed us away from a casual view of sin and reawakened our lost sense of awe. I still resonated to the idea of a God of power who actually does what He says. I wanted to extend my new evangelical vocabulary, but I still longed for the God of the miraculous.

As we took the last photographs, exchanged telephone numbers and promised to keep in touch, I had no better idea where I was going than I had on that first day three years earlier. I did have some good interim plans, but as I headed home with my small huddle of family and friends it seemed that this was only another milestone on my pilgrimage.

4

Mind the Gap

The first four months after leaving London Bible College were very strange. Having left with no set plans I had followed my general inclination to become a probation officer by sending off an application for a position as an ancillary worker. For some time I had thought that I might work with young people in the criminal justice system. It was an idea which had never really left me during my time at LBC but, equally, I had no set thoughts about it being a career until shortly after my graduation.

Having applied to the Inner London Probation and After Care Service I entered the waiting game. It was a long summer withdrawing from academic life and getting back to the real world. It was strange being home again and feeling the claustrophobia of our small council flat in Woodbury Downs. And what could I do with the words and ideas poured in over three intensive years which made no sense to those around me now? My three years away had been a major social and educational transformation which my family and friends at home had not shared. Inevitably it meant that we began to see the world differently. It had nothing to do with being better than anyone else; it was simply that we now had very different frames of reference. It was rather like travelling to a far country and seeing new colours. How can anyone describe new colours?

But it meant enjoying the familiarities of home again without term-time interruptions, though I also realised that parts of the new me were likely to be partitioned off from family life. Meal-time conversations were unlikely to focus on the finer points of Luther's understanding of grace or the classic arguments for the existence of God. In real terms domestic conversations were hardly different from before I went away.

I had become more questioning, though, and others noticed. It showed up more in the local church. I was something of a misfit who was frequently misunderstood but greatly loved. There was no doubt about it: the people among whom I had grown up and who stood by me, were very proud of what I had achieved. A degree in theology was rare in the Black church community of the early 1970s. But I had little idea how to handle the responsibilities of this privileged position in the early stages of my return to my spiritual home. Re-entry into the world of Black Pentecostalism after the rarefied atmosphere of suburban student life happened without any coaching.

The pastor who had pointed me towards Northwood, and who had a very good grasp of the issues raised by the experience of study, had emigrated to America shortly after my departure to LBC. It soon became evident to me in those early months that the tools of detached analysis were more likely to be understood as a threat than a service. I learned the importance of becoming a good listener – even if I thought I had the answers. I was pleased to be back in church again but I soon realised that things weren't what they used to be.

The most difficult part of the period between leaving college and starting my first job four months later was simply the waiting. I had never had such a drawn-out period of inactivity and uncertainty. For the first time I understood how people without work could become lethargic and depressed.

My great consolation was my growing relationship with Carol. I first saw her at our Clapton branch in east London in 1969. The weekend meeting attracted a number of our sister churches from throughout the London area who visited for the Sunday afternoon programme. During the session a group from the church in Brixton went up to sing and I spotted her. We met later that year at our National Convention in Leicester and by the time I went to LBC in 1972 we had the beginning of a somewhat uncertain relationship which hung together during my time away and her training as a nurse in Kent.

During the difficult time of waiting for work, the one emerging certainty was our growing relationship which had taken on the shape of a more confident courtship by this stage. Carol and I were married in my home church in May 1976. But before we were married I found a job. I had my interview to join the Probation Service in October 1975. It was my second experience of an interview and it did not start off very well. I had been surprised to find the office situated right next to the Magistrates' Court, but my main interviewer explained that it was quite common, given the close working relationship between the courts and the Probation Service. She went on to dispel a few more myths about the Service: it was not mainly to do with children; that had been changed by a Children and Young Persons Act a few years earlier. A good deal of the work would involve working with adults and even with marriage problems where the custody of children was to be decided through the courts. As an ancillary worker I would be working with the officers to help them do a professional job and it would be an ideal window into the nature and scope of the profession.

They did wonder what made me come to the Probation

Service having studied theology. But I suggested that the Bible was profoundly concerned with human relationships and that theology was as good a preparation for this kind of work as anything else. They liked me, and the fact that I was a young Black male was probably very helpful in a period when the service was becoming very aware that it was receiving a disproportionate number of Black youngsters through the courts.

I was not a complete stranger to the courts system, but my previous experience could have counted against me rather than advancing my career. In my first year of secondary school I had been in trouble with the law. Along with another pupil I was caught stealing from Woolworth's. I had developed a steady business of stealing small items from the store and trading them at school. Eventually I was caught and taken to the local police station. It was, without doubt, one of the worst moments of my life. Eventually, the horrific silence of the police cell was broken by my mother's distraught and tearful arrival. I appeared at the Juvenile Court, was placed on a year's supervision order but never ever saw anyone from the Probation Service. I have no idea how it became possible for me to drift into a life of petty crime for I had maintained a regular and active church life. Somehow, I had fallen into a double lifestyle which seemed fun while it lasted, but was very bitter when I woke from it in the coldness of the police cell.

And now here I was about to start my professional life as a probation officer. I worked for eighteen months as an ancillary worker before leaving to study for two years to gain a Certificate of Qualification in Social Work at Middlesex Polytechnic. The contrast between the polytechnic and LBC could not have been more marked. Life at Middlesex was like being thrown around by tidal waves of confused values in an ocean of intellectual arrogance. For two years we were blown around by the free winds of secular humanism with little idea where firm ground was to be found. I was glad to leave and accept a place as a probation officer with the Inner London Probation Service in 1977.

I'm certain that my negative response to Middlesex had a great deal to do with my own intellectual unpreparedness for the course. It seemed that I had been given very few tools, either from my earlier study or indeed from my church experience, to prepare me to fight the intellectual and philosophical battles of secular humanism. Up to that point so much of what I had learned about God had very little to do with the sort of things I was being faced with in the topsy-turvy world beyond my Christian environment. But even though I felt ill equipped to dismantle the towers of secular thought, I knew instinctively that much of what I was seeing and hearing was profoundly mistaken.

My work in the Probation Service itself helped me come to that conclusion. For eight and a half years I worked as a field officer in North Islington supervising a range of client groups, including young offenders. In family custody cases I helped the magistrates determine which parent should have responsibility for their children following separation or divorce. The message became very clear: left to our own devices we go wrong. The problem which the Bible calls 'sin' was openly exhibited. It was evident, too, that the social experiment of human self-determination had serious social flaws and that neither policy makers, social scientists, social workers nor our clients really demonstrated any real ability to solve the problems we were all struggling to overcome. Usually, we were applying cosmetics when radical surgery was needed.

My last eighteen months as a probation officer were on a part-time basis at Holloway Prison for women. It was the most painful time of my professional life in the Probation Service. I met vulnerable and broken women who were being further damaged in the name of justice. Every day it became more evident to me that law and justice were not the same thing. It was a case of the good, the bad and the sad all thrown together. I met women from Africa and Latin America, arrested at airports for trafficking drugs. Several had no knowledge of their children's welfare but were so ashamed that they did not want their families to know where they were. For many of these women, this kind of 'work' was the only alternative to prostitution if they were to provide for their children in desperate circumstances. Others, through their own naivety, had been duped into trafficking, either through family members or casual friends. I have often thought about one retired Black woman and her daughter-in-law who went on holiday to the Caribbean. They were found to have a quantity of cannabis when they returned to Heathrow. Neither of them had ever had any dealings with the police before and prided themselves on their hitherto crime-free lifestyle. Both were devastated by their conviction. Their hair fell out and they were totally mesmerised by the system. What made the case particularly pathetic was that the elderly prisoner, who had lived and worked in the UK for over thirty years, could not identify the name of the drug she was carrying. There were few prisoners or prison officers who argued her guilt.

Not all prisoners had the same kind of virtue. Young prostitutes, desperate for genuine love and caught in a tangled web of drug addiction and slave-sex to keep their pimps going, were thrown together with petty thieves and women who had taken other people's lives. In separate blocks, prisoners who had committed crimes like child murders were contained for their own safety. As terrible as some of these crimes were, I was always curious to meet the real women behind the newspaper headlines.

As in all penal institutions, justice and injustice met at Holloway Prison. The idea of God's grace began to make more sense. I had preached a lot about God's 'unmerited favour' and I knew, from my own conversion and God's restoration, the strength of that grace in my own life. But in Holloway, with its intense dramatisation of human failure, of pain and the fallibility of human justice all around me, I understood better the need for a justice based on the truth of a God before whom everything is open knowledge. In Holloway my job was not to treat the prisoners according to their guilt but to treat them as people. I and my colleagues were arbitrators to the outside world. We made their powerlessness bearable and provided the same service for the guilty and innocent. At times it was uncomfortable to find that I liked a woman accused of murdering her infant. In a way incomprehensible to the newspaper reader I shared the pain of the inner prison created by her own guilt or denial. It was humbling to recognise that if I stood in a line-up with any of these women, God would love them as much as He loved me.

It seemed to me that in this environment the Bible was about being honest rather than just. Great desperate wrongs either make it so difficult for people to face up to our capacity to be so evil or make it very easy to retreat into dishonesty about the implications of what we have done. This must have been Adam's psychological problem. God's response was to encourage him to be honest. Confession is the ultimate level of honesty which empowers us to face our ultimate wrong called 'sin'.

One prisoner, later extradited to the States for the double murder of her parents, found this to be the case. Elizabeth agreed with her German boyfriend to commit the crime. After months of escape through drugs and international travel they were finally tracked down in London. We met in Holloway when she was ready to be honest. She found the Bible a helpful tool. Her honesty cost her a total of ninety-nine years' imprisonment.

My time as a probation officer and my work in Holloway,

in particular, showed me that honest truth is not aggressive. It starts off with an advantage, for it appeals to the deeply known facts about ourselves. It does not need to shout. It merely challenges us to be honest and leaves us with the implications of our own choice. My Holloway experience told me that no one in their right mind could deny either the reality of human sinfulness or our own inability to help ourselves. But it also taught me that God knows us in the intimacy of our own fears and imprisonments and loves us in spite of the headlines we create for ourselves.

Outside work, church life took a momentous turn in 1985. It began with a telephone call one evening in the summer of 1985 when our national superintendent, Selwyn Arnold, rang me at home. There was a small church of thirty-five people who needed a new pastor and the executive were inviting me to consider the post. I had not thought of being a pastor and I knew very little about the church, but I accepted.

Leaving my old church in Willesden was very traumatic. It was the place of my spiritual birth and belonging. By this stage I had learned much more about humility, patience and servanthood. It had not been a particularly easy time of transition after my return from college but both Carol and I were very secure in the church, enjoying the confidence of the congregation and providing a significant level of informal support for many of the youngsters in the fellowship. But we also knew it was time to go. We began our ministry in Mile End New Testament Church of God on 1 September 1985.

It soon became evident that our work in Mile End was unlikely to be typical of our denominational brand. Evidently the very traditional approach of my predecessor had limitations. We came to a congregation which was ready for change and brought to it our own pilgrimage experience which could not settle with the status quo. Too many questions had been locked away in my own mind about the things we deemed to be important. I had long lost confidence in an approach to church which emphasised external matters at the expense of internal discipline, holiness and relevance to the rest of the world. I felt, too, that as an African–Caribbean congregation we still needed to develop a consciousness about the wider cultural context of the East End without losing our own identity.

Perhaps the most powerful influence on my ministry in Mile End was the daily contact which I had with the community through my full-time work as a professional social worker. It was impossible to see church people – especially the younger members of the congregation – as different from the community beyond the church walls. The most immediate influence on my preaching was the contact I had with my clients. They reminded me that church people were a part of the real world too. All too frequently I saw myself or members of my own congregation in the human predicaments of my clients. I knew we had added resources of grace to help us through the everyday difficulties and that the Holy Spirit was in so many ways so present to empower, but I also learned that our humanity is real and the Bible needed to say something which still made sense on weekdays as well as Sundays.

Our experiment in relevance led us to take risks based on a conviction that God was bigger than we were used to thinking. Because we believed that God was bigger than our own church we had to behave accordingly. I preached about Jesus, His work and His cross. We focused on the need for discipleship, fellowship and worship. We tried to become more involved in our community. We reminded ourselves about the work of the Holy Spirit for believers and the Church and tried to help everyone understand the great themes of forgiveness, justification and holiness. We also taught about the distinctive characteristics of our denomination. But in all of this we struggled to separate our own prejudgments about what it meant to be a Christian from what we saw in the Bible. We did not mention much about dress codes and did not preach prescriptive sermons about where people should not go at weekends.

At times our work was lonely as we sought to be real rather than predictable. It was plain that we had to learn how to identify and communicate the priorities of the Gospel in ways which were not bound by the cultural definitions of a 1960s Caribbean mindset, which meant little to younger Black British Christians or to those attempting to put down drawbridges to a wider culture.

By this time I had further opportunities to work within the wider Church through itinerant ministry and involvement in the early stages of Spring Harvest, which was to go on to become the largest Christian teaching conference in Europe. Leadership '84, hosted by the Evangelical Alliance, also gave me a brief reintroduction to the wider world of British evangelicalism from which I had become somewhat detached since leaving college.

But by 1987 I was becoming very restless. There was no logical reason for it. Most things were going very well. By this stage Carol and I had two children: Joel and Davina were nine and six. We were in our second year in the leadership of a small church branch in east London. The unnatural restlessness was particularly pronounced in my work as a probation officer. I could have done well in the Service and there were many voices encouraging me to consider promotion. But I could not stay. It was the same restlessness I had experienced in my home church in Willesden shortly before I was invited to take up the pastoral work in Mile End. It was simply time to go.

It was about this time that I first met Phillip Mohabir during a week spent together at Spring Harvest in

Minehead. It wasn't long before I discovered that this man had a very big heart for missions and reconciliation. He told me how God had called him from Guyana in the Caribbean as a missionary to Britain in the 1950s. I laughed but he kept a straight face. Phillip had played a significant role in the formative stages of the Black church presence in Britain and also built very close relationships with many of the New Churches, which he had maintained during his return to the Caribbean. His international ministry and love for reconciliation led him back to the United Kingdom in the early 1980s. On returning to the UK, he was encouraged to see the significant growth of the evangelical witness in general and the Evangelical Alliance in particular. What surprised him was the wide gulf which still existed between the White churches and the rapidly growing Black churches.

Phillip worked together with a number of key Black church leaders to form a ministry with a twofold purpose: to build stronger links between the disparate Black church groups and to work for reconciliation with White evangelicals. In April 1984 the West Indian Evangelical Alliance had been born.

The conversation with Phillip was exciting. For me this development about which I had only the vaguest notion was the model of things I had long felt convinced about. A few months later, the still fledgling organisation, working in partnership with the Evangelical Alliance, invited me to become its first General Secretary, working alongside Phillip as its founding Chairman.

I started work with the West Indian Evangelical Alliance in February 1988. It meant leaving my job-share as a probation officer in Holloway Prison and dividing my time between pastoral work and my new job as General Secretary of WIEA. My first formal meeting with the WIEA council was at Phillip's home in Brixton. It included some people I knew before, as well as some new faces. My arrival was warmly welcomed because he was already too busy with the growing demands of his international ministry. The council was happy that I remain a local pastor, giving two and a half days a week to WIEA. They were clearly committed to a movement which drew together the Black church community to represent its concerns to the wider community and also to build strong links with the growing evangelical Church in Britain. It was to be a flagship for reconciliation between Black and White evangelicals. I felt very privileged to be asked to take on this role because it resonated so much with my own long-standing convictions.

Shortly after my initial meeting with the WIEA council I met Clive Calver, who was the General Secretary of the Evangelical Alliance at the time. It was my second meeting with him. Our first meeting was outside the front gate at Caister for Leadership '84. As I approached the main entrance I noticed him, clutching a walkie-talkie, welcoming a number of people. Before I had a chance to say hello he greeted me by my name. I was very struck by the encounter.

My new role also meant that I was joining the leadership team of the Evangelical Alliance as a mark of our integral partnership. It was a brand new chapter for me. In effect it was an opportunity to work through many of my own convictions about the Black Christian presence in Britain and to explore ways in which greater unity could be forged between the African–Caribbean churches. WIEA was not the only or oldest ministry which set out to work across the Caribbean constituency, but it was the first which stood in a clearly evangelical partnership with a commitment to work towards reconciliation.

The Black Church in Britain is a curious phenomenon in British church life. It began in the mid 1950s with the early wave of immigrants from the Commonwealth who were invited to post-war Britain to rebuild the depleted transport, national health and manual industries. Significant numbers of Caribbeans came to the UK with vibrant faith; most of them were from the historic denominations, but sadly many of these individuals were not welcomed by their fellow Christians and the fall-out from the historic churches was, in part, the reason which gave rise to the rumours in the Caribbean that England was a spiritual graveyard.

But the influx of Caribbeans also gave rise to growing numbers of Pentecostal churches. In the face of marginal-isation many Black Christians left the established churches. But it is also likely that many of them would have done so in any case. The Christian culture of 1950s Britain was alien to the new Christians from the Caribbean. It was far more secular and theologically compromised than they were accustomed to. They were uncomfortable about bishops and senior church leaders who denied central historic doctrines, and felt distanced by the sophisticated worship even where the liturgy was familiar to them.

In this environment, the growing presence of Black Pentecostal faith was unlikely to sit at ease with the pre-renewal ethos of British church life. Pentecostals arriving from the Caribbean between 1950 and 1980 lacked the liturgical polish of their British counterparts. Generally, they were noisier, preached considerably longer and had quite different expectations of the worship experience.

But they also had very different needs which could not readily be met by indigenous Christians. Cultural belonging, so needed in those early times, could only be provided by the Black Church itself. The Caribbean Church, like many other cultures since, was forced to provide its own cultural continuity sustained in the worship context. It was not long before the denominational distinctives from the Caribbean replicated themselves in the UK. What began as closely knit friendships and fellowships among Caribbean church leaders rapidly re-grouped along old denominational loyalties, with new groups emerging out of personality conflicts and fresh initiatives. Before long, Caribbean Christianity in Britain had become as diverse as our British counterparts with its historic groups and New Church developments of the 1960s and 1970s.

It became evident that the presence of African Christianity in Britain would present WIEA with a new challenge of reconciliation. Before Black consciousness of the 1960s and the growing Afro-centric movements of the late 1970s, most Caribbean Christians were unwilling to be linked to an African identity. In an effort to respond positively to this development WIEA became the African and Caribbean Evangelical Alliance (ACEA) and sought to work across the African and Caribbean divide.

It was not an easily understood concept and we were invariably presented with searching questions about ACEA's work. Some Black Christians were clearly suspicious about a partnership between Black and White Christians which appeared to suggest that there was a dependency on White evangelicals. Many noted that, historically, evangelicals were not very good at championing matters of social justice and were less visibly involved in empowering minorities in comparison with ecumenical bodies such as the World Council of Churches and the Council of Churches in Britain and Ireland. One of our greatest battles with Black Christians in seeking reconciliation was to convince some church leaders that the work we were doing did not amount to a new White evangelical imperialism. We had to argue that ACEA was not a doctrinal 'sell out' to apostasy or questionable morality. At the outset only a very small part of the Black Church understood the need or wisdom of working closer with White evangelicalism. Most were content to paddle their own self-determined course in a relatively small and sometimes diminishing pond. Others were unimpressed with the track record of declining numbers which typified British Christianity in contrast with their own growing and time-consuming work. A much smaller number had the ambassadorial consciousness which saw the need for relationships with the wider body of Christ.

Yet again, some Black Christians shared the view of some White evangelicals that the idea of a separate 'Black Alliance' was a kind of Christian apartheid. It was a point made to me with some force during a brief visit to South Africa in 1989. It was a very natural line of argument: if we are all one in Christ, why do we need a separate Alliance for Black Christians? Should we not be together without distinctions?

ACEA's commitment to partnership was twofold. Its first focus was to bring together the growing and diverse groups of Black churches around a common vision in order to build strong bonds with the wider evangelical presence in the UK. It was unlikely to happen without a focal point around the common issues and concerns facing Black Christians and in an environment where Black church leaders trusted the security of things and people who were familiar to them. ACEA had come into being to build a community of Christians who would, from a position of corporate strength, build lasting relationships with its wider evangelical family. It was a responsibility it could not ignore. The guiding vision was to build dual reconciliation without losing its essential character.

And there was reconciliation to be done between our various groups. My own denomination, the New Testament Church of God, was always ill at ease with the Church of God of Prophecy. Although both groups had a great deal in common, minor differences and the history of our common founder in America, A.J. Tomlinson, led to mutual suspicion. Church of God of Prophecy do not formally allow their women to wear wedding bands and we do. And

Tomlinson, we claim, first established the Church of God before defecting to found Prophecy – and they have a reverse history! Even though as youngsters we shared a common interest in Gospel concerts, the protocol was clear: Prophecy and Church of God do not mix.

Shortly after beginning my work in ACEA I learned that the Church of God of Prophecy had appointed a new leader. I had had little success in contacting his predecessor despite a number of attempts to do so. The new leader, Ossie Williams, was about my age. Appointed at the age of thirty-nine, he was unusually young for the post. I decided to cross the barrier and visited Ossie at his office in Birmingham. It didn't take us long to discover that we had a great deal in common. Both of us had very real concerns about the historic divide between our churches which seemed to be out of all proportion to the things we shared. Together we discussed the serious challenges facing Black church leaders and the potential for greater effectiveness which would come with more combined efforts. As we concluded our time together Ossie asked if I knew of a conference centre for his forthcoming ministers' meeting. I mentioned that our denomination had a conference facility in Northampton but equally recognised that that might not be appropriate. I was pleasantly surprised to learn some weeks later that the Church of God of Prophecy had booked Northampton to have their next ministers' conference.

It is one example among many which demonstrates how much movement towards unity has actually taken place among Black churches in recent years, not only through the work of ACEA but as the result of other friends and organisations who have been prepared to come together around common aims on behalf of our members and the wider community. Surprisingly, very little of this has had anything to do with shifts in theological perceptions. In the main it has been the result of a willingness to listen and to allow for the fact that we still have something to learn from others around us.

In its formative stages we set out to identify those specific needs of the African–Caribbean community which were as yet unmet. A range of activities were devised to meet the specific theological perceptions and experiences of the African–Caribbean church. ACEA hosted special meetings for Black ministers and receptions for Black and White Christian leaders together. In 1990 we introduced ACCORD, which lasted four years, and although it was short-lived it expressed the objective of a cross-denominational setting in which Black and White Christians met at a nationwide event hosted by the Black Christian community.

After four years I became restless again. Once again it didn't make sense. I felt I understood the agenda for ACEA which we had carefully formulated. I had made significant progress in winning the confidence of church leaders in the Black churches and had forged meaningful relationships with evangelical leaders throughout the UK. ACEA had in fact provided something of a model for working relationships within the Evangelical Alliance as a whole, with the development of Alliances in Wales and Northern Ireland in 1989 and Scotland in 1990. Unknown to most people around me it was becoming very difficult to motivate myself to continue the work. More than ever I had a clear commitment to reconciliation and a passion to discover just what God was doing beyond my own backyard. The work in ACEA seemed to give me the opportunity to do so. The silent restlessness was out of step with my heart.

In 1992 the Evangelical Alliance was going through a major change in its leadership. Ian Coffey, a fellow student at LBC and the Field Director since 1988, was due to take up the pastorate at Mutley Baptist Church in

Plymouth. The Alliance had grown in its role and profile across the UK. As General Director, Clive Calver's work in the media had grown significantly. It was an opportune time to reshape EA's leadership and I was invited to consider joining a newly shaped leadership team as EA's Director of UK Development – a job title which later became UK Director under Clive's leadership as General Director.

My task was to facilitate and stimulate better relationships within our diverse membership, dealing with some difficult membership issues, organising EA's council meetings and co-ordinating the working relationships between EA's central team and the Alliances in the Celtic nations.

My immediate response was ambivalent. There seemed to be so much to do in ACEA, and in any event I simply was not expecting this scale of involvement in British evangelicalism. It took a good deal of thought and prayerful reflection to help me recognise that it was right to respond to this invitation.

While I was finally dithering on the brink of my decision, I was pushed over the edge by a quite extraordinary event. Late on a Friday evening in the late spring of 1992 I went for an informal meeting with members of the EA executive to discuss the invitation. I left informing them that I would give the matter some final thoughts. Very early the following morning I left my home to attend a conference of the Foursquare Church at Kinmel Hall in Wales. During the evening worship service a woman I had never met approached me, saying that God wanted to speak to me. We went to a quiet area where we could hear each other. She appeared very nervous and I encouraged her to say what she felt she had to say.

'During the worship,' she began, 'I saw a green light over your head. God says to tell you that you must go! God says to tell you that He is about to change your ministry and you will be travelling a lot more than you used to do.' My knees almost gave way. She kept going. 'God says to tell you that He admires you and, because you have walked softly before Him, He will lift you up.'

I learned afterwards that her name was Marianne and she was the wife of Henk Rothuizen of the Rafael Foursquare Church in Holland. I tried to think of ways in which she may have known about my meeting the previous day but none of them seemed remotely likely. I decided to accept the job – I knew it was entirely consistent with what I felt God was leading me to do. My formal role as UK Director began the following September.

5

Tribes and Traditions

Marianne's prophetic statement swiftly came to fruition. I joined a delegation to the World Evangelical Fellowship Assembly in Manila in June. It was my very first introduction to the global evangelical community. The opportunity to be a part of an international gathering of evangelicals came at a very opportune time in my work with the Alliance as it opened up an awareness that evangelicalism was an international movement. The conference was particularly significant as it marked a change of leadership from David Howard from the United States to the movement's first non-American, Jun Vencer, whose Philippine Council of Evangelical Churches (PCEC) hosted the assembly. In the poverty and political turmoil of the Philippines I saw for the first time the transforming impact of an evangelical witness committed to community and political involvement.

It was intriguing that this experience had come so quickly upon me as I was preparing to take up my formal role within the Alliance in September. Both had given me a wider canvas for an understanding of the diversity of evangelical Christianity throughout the world.

Once my appointment was formally announced I felt swept away by the wave of approval which came from a wide range of Christian friends and members of the

Alliance. It seemed as though a number of people were waiting for it to happen. I was particularly overwhelmed by the affirmation which came from the Alliances in Scotland, Northern Ireland and Wales. A significant part of my responsibility as the new UK Director was to facilitate good relationships between the national Alliances and the 'central UK' Alliance. Having partnered the development of the fledgling Alliances we recognised the need to support the distinctives of each Alliance, working with their general secretaries, councils and executives. This balance of responsibilities, held together by agreed parameters, mutual trust and respect for diversity, was to be an integral part of my role within the UK Alliance. For me it was particularly gratifying that our colleagues in the Celtic nations and the Province vicariously identified themselves in my appointment and seemed to enjoy an enhanced sense of confidence in what we were modelling together.

On my first visit to the Scottish Evangelical Alliance in October 1992, as the plane taxied towards the runway at Heathrow, I couldn't help reflecting on how much had happened in a short space of time. It was the latest in a number of long-distance trips I had made since agreeing to take up the challenge of the new task. But it wasn't the plane ride which gave me a sense of exhilaration. It was the recognition that I had made the right decision. Earlier visits to the Alliances in Wales and Northern Ireland left me in no doubt that what we were pioneering in evangelical diversity was worth doing – even though we were all learning daily by our mistakes.

The Alliance had by now raised a huge banner for evangelical unity in diversity. We had done so not only by our rhetoric but also by our programmes and priorities. For years as General Director, Clive Calver presented the Alliance as an 'umbrella' under which the various 'tribes of evangelicalism' could meet to work for the good of society, or as a 'table-top' on which the jigsaw pieces of our diverse communities could come together. This pan-evangelical vision had shown itself by its participation in giving birth to Spring Harvest, Europe's largest Christian teaching conference, in two significant leadership meetings in 1984 and 1989 and in numerous coalitions bringing together specialists and church leaders around specific issues.

That same October the Alliance made its most significant gesture for evangelical unity with the opening of Whitefield House as an evangelical centre. To some extent, the decision was forced upon us by necessity. Rapid growth and the increasing profile of the ministry meant that it outgrew its twin-sited arrangement in Kennington. After considerable thought about relocation, we were drawn to the idea of an evangelical centre both to provide adequate accommodation for the work and also to offer a conference facility and a meeting point for evangelicals. On 3 October the centre was formally opened with a special service of dedication in Westminster Central Hall.

Within a few weeks, it was becoming evident that a familiar cycle in evangelicalism was taking place. Evangelical growth was in danger of coming apart at the seams. A small group of the Alliance's council and staff met to discuss the danger of fragmentation within evangelical Christianity. The discussion took place against the backdrop of several key events. Anglicans were debating the issue of women's ordination; tensions were growing over visits from American evangelists such as Morris Cerullo and Benny Hinn who drew the attention of the Christian press. While we were still getting over the questions raised by the visit of the Kansas City prophets in 1992, the evangelical world was caught off-guard by the surprise friendship of Paul Caine, a controversial prophetic figure from the United States, and Rev. Dr R.T. Kendall, minister of Westminster Chapel, who shared the platform under the theme 'Word and Spirit', hosted at Wembley Conference Centre by a group of north London churches called 'Beulah'. Not only did the two men get on very well but they declared themselves to be friends and Kendall informed the conference that Paul Caine was a member of the Chapel! It was for Kendall, a well-known reformed Bible teacher, one of the most controversial episodes of his ministry in the UK.

The writing was already on the wall. Unless evangelicals made a deliberate effort to address the issues which could potentially divide there was every danger that the strength of the biblical witness built up over many years would be undermined. By the time I came to my new role such a response was already in motion.

For some months before my appointment the Evangelical Alliance and the British Evangelical Alliance planned to resuscitate a defunct forum which had fallen by the wayside over fifteen years before. The Evangelical Leaders' Forum pulled together a small group of senior evangelical leaders from a wide range of theological and cultural positions for a forty-eight-hour, private meeting. Many of them had not met before. Others had strained relationships. The first of three bi-annual meetings took place in a small hotel in Nuneaton in May 1993 with twenty-five leaders discussing evangelical unity. It was in fact one of my first significant and fairly sensitive tasks as UK Director. As host, and in view of my own responsibilities within the Alliance, I was asked to present a paper in the penultimate session on 'Overcoming Barriers and Being Facilitators of Good Practice and United Work'. It was the longest theme I had ever been offered and one of the most daunting since being invited to preach on the Second Coming as a teenager! My presentation amounted to a personal account of my own journey, identifying the landmarks in my own theological, cultural and spiritual development. I was somewhat taken aback to discover that it had so many parallels for others. What became very evident was that although there were genuine and deeply felt differences there was still a good deal which united this diverse group of people.

The Forum, though sensitive, proved very positive. It registered two very important things for me. The first was the recognition that as a diverse group of leaders, we came not only with our different theological perceptions and experiences but equally with different stories. We each spoke of our commitment to truth and our longing for unity; it was a united voice but with many different accents. This realisation encouraged me to adapt my presentation to the Forum accordingly. It was based simply on my own pilgrimage up to that point. It was the story of my life.

My second lesson came from Ian Coffey. As we discussed thorny issues about unity from our varied perspectives Ian said: 'What we need is a theology of diversity.' It struck me as something worth thinking about.

The modern evangelical movement has been issued periodical reminders of its 'tribal distinctives'. In 1994, for example, Spring Harvest focused on the 'Twelve Tribes', drawing material from an earlier publication of the Alliance, *Who Do Evangelicals Think They Are?* (E.A. Publications). The same thoughts were reflected by Clive Calver and Rob Warner in *Together We Stand* (Hodder & Stoughton, 1996). Derek Tidball's helpful historical review, *Who are the Evangelicals?* (Marshall Pickering, 1994), provided us with a Rubik Cube approach to evangelicalism, showing various perspectives around three important issues: the world, spirituality and our understanding of church.

It is probably significant that evangelicalism has been so preoccupied with definitions. The broader Christian community has certainly raised important questions about the nature of church. Consequently, ecumenism – the world-wide movement of a broad fellowship of Christian groups including Protestants, Orthodox and Catholics – has been less prescriptive and much more inclusive in its approach to Christian fellowship than most evangelical groups. Ecumenism has been committed to the recovery of a theology of Christian pilgrimage and prepared to work within a wider doctrinal framework than evangelical Christians. The breadth of biblical positions within ecumenical groups has often presented evangelicals with a dilemma in discussing wider Christian relationships. If the truth be told, the sticking point for evangelicals committed to the principles of the Reformation has been the involvement of Catholic Christians in ecumenism.

It is worth bearing in mind, too, that evangelicalism can also lay claim to being the oldest expression of ecumenical Christianity. The Evangelical Alliance launched in 1846 was at that time the widest expression of Christian diversity, as some nine hundred Christian leaders from around the world met in London to give expression to their united commitment to the relevance and credibility of the Bible in their contemporary culture. It was a dream for an international alliance which floundered in the first instance although it gave birth to the Evangelical Alliance in Britain.

Evangelicalism has been no stranger to the notion of diversity. The practice has always been difficult. It became clear to me that it would remain an important element of my work in the years ahead. It was difficult, not only because it led us from time to time to look at contentious issues facing us but because I was constantly being forced to separate my own prejudices from my convictions. My clear convictions did not always help me to answer all the questions adequately.

My first visit to the European Charismatic Conference in Berne, Switzerland, had been in 1990. It was a surcharge of the unusual. In the heady days immediately after the fall of communism, the large gathering of charismatic ecumenicals was euphoric about the significant presence of Eastern Europeans emerging from behind the Iron Curtain to tell us of miraculous stories of faithfulness and miracles. I sat with numerous individuals whose stories overwhelmed me. Persecuted and harassed, they had held firm to their faith in Christ. Imprisoned and dispossessed, they did not give way to the hostilities of communist dictators. They had come out of it with evident love for God, personal devotion to Christ and testimonies of the work of the Holy Spirit. We were enriched by them and they were encouraged by us. All around me were thousands of fellow delegates who all laid claim to 'being filled with the Spirit', spoke in tongues and evidently exercised gifts of the Spirit, understood their Bibles and loved God. It would have been so much easier if so many of them had not been Catholic and if others of them did not smoke during the intermissions.

In October 1993 my Berne experience was followed up by a smaller consultation of European charismatics in Hungary. Members of the Dutch Reformed Church mingled with Catholics, New Church members, historic traditions, Orthodox charismatics and Pentecostals. We discussed theological issues, missions and the growth of charismatics in Europe.

I had heard about this confusion of charismatic ecumenism. It was a fairly cut and dried issue. The whole thing, critics said, was entirely about experience at the expense of theological thought. There was bound to be something defective in the experience itself growing as it must from a defective and compromised theological position. Furthermore, it was impossible to think of any genuine experience of the Holy Spirit among Catholics who embraced Rome. These were reasonable fears for a Black Pentecostal. My Pentecostal upbringing made me well disposed towards a gentle anti-Rome hostility. For many of us, our pre-millennium position made it easy to see the Pope and all members of Roman Catholicism as the Anti-Christ. My problem was that not all Catholics saw the papacy the same way. None of them had the 'Mary phobia' of Protestantism and none of those I met were prepared to place her above Christ. Everyone I came across agreed with the doctrine of justification by faith and the process of conversion.

I could not bring myself to understand how Bible Christians could remain in a church which had never formally reviewed its response to the Reformation doctrine of justification by faith or the position of Mary and its teaching about purgatory. But I did learn that Catholicism was not a monolithic movement in which everyone swore blind obedience to the idea of papal infallibility, and that Orthodox Christians should be taken more seriously.

We avoided taking communion in either of these settings in case it caused offence. That in itself was a very important comment about the nature of the events. For both settings there were easy answers. My answers did not become irrelevant in the face of this experience of diversity; it was just that they did not fit as comfortably in the reality of the situation. It was not as easy to say that I disagree with Catholics, even though it remained as easy to say that I had difficulties with Catholicism. I remained unconvinced about many aspects of ecumenism – even a charismatic ecumenism – but it did leave me wondering whether 'evangelical' could be a reliable synonym for 'Christian'.

In this breadth of Christian experience and genuine encounters with the Holy Spirit there was an untidiness about God which became strangely disconcerting. It re-minded me of my visit to South Africa. Evangelical Support for South Africa was a group which the Alliance facilitated in the closing years of the apartheid regime. Our main point of contact was through Caesar Mollebatsie, a Black South African who suffered personally under the injustices of apartheid and who travelled extensively to raise the agenda beyond South Africa. In 1989, a few months before the release of Nelson Mandela, I was one of eight church leaders from Europe and America who visited the country under Caesar's invitation. It was during this memorable visit that we met with Frank Chikane. Frank, who was then the General Secretary of the ecumenical South African Council of Churches, was also a minister with the Apostolic Pentecostal Church in South Africa who experienced severe persecution, not only from the South African authorities but also directly through White police officers from his own church whom he knew personally. In our private meeting with him we asked how it was possible for him as a classical Pentecostal to find himself as the leader of the ecumenical movement in South Africa.

His timely response was recklessly honest. 'When you are in prison with a Roman Catholic,' he said, 'you do not discuss transubstantiation!'

It was during this period of my own ministry that I was drawn to two Pentecostal giants, David Du Plessis and Donald Gee. Both were Pentecostal pioneering ecumenists in very different ways. Du Plessis, also known as Mr Pentecost, was a South African whose ministry had been launched by one of the twentieth century's most prominent Pentecostals, Smith Wigglesworth. Wigglesworth prophesied that Du Plessis would be an international figure in church relationships, and he turned out to be the first international Pentecostal ecumenist whose contacts ranged from the free independent churches to the historic denominations, including Catholicism. The breadth of Du Plessis' ministry has certainly compromised his memory with many Pentecostals who strongly disagreed with his ecumenical links, but there is no doubting his stature as a leading Pentecostal figure. Donald Gee was an Assemblies of God minister who had the foresight to see that Pentecostalism, pressed as it was by the hostilities of the older Christian traditions, could easily become a reactionary and defensive group. He issued a famous 'Nother Springtime' speech, appealing to Pentecostals to adopt a wider view of the Christian Church than they might otherwise have adopted.

As a Pentecostal minister learning to respond to the demands of a wider ministry I found Colin Whittaker's excerpt from Gee's chairman's address to the Assemblies of God conference in 1960 very moving:

A new era appears to be dawning for that Revival of the manifestations of the Holy Spirit that for the last fifty years has been associated almost exclusively with the Pentecostal Movement. Can we rise by the grace of God to the challenge and responsibility of a new situation? We must shed our complexes, bred by the ostracism of half a century, and boldly take our place alongside our brethren in Christ in the older denominations who may now surprise us by their openness to new movings of God's Spirit. To share in such a new Springtime of Pentecostal grace and power will be thrilling.

It was as though this speech had been lodged in my mind for years and was now being called up to conscious recognition. For many Pentecostals of his day this challenge would have been a very difficult idea to embrace. For many today, it still remains a problem.

Increasingly it occurred to me that our Christian commitment and ministries could never be conducted in airtight containers without reference to those other parts of the Christian community with which we are uncomfortable. Christian faith has never been tidy and any attempt to produce a clinical code of theological prescriptions which answers all the questions was bound to be driven either by a polemic existence, by which I defended my own positions against the rest of the Christian world, or a theology of insecurity which is afraid to talk to anyone with whom I happen to disagree. In the interest of defending truth and the Bible many sincere Christians also become deaf to possibilities beyond their own terms of reference.

It is a posture which is understandable given the relativism of modern thought by which all values have been reduced to our own convenient preferences. The late Lesslie Newbigin told the story of a young man who was asked to name the capital city of Pakistan and said that he wasn't sure and would therefore keep an open mind on the subject! There are some things about which biblical Christianity simply cannot be open to all possibilities. The tough task of serious biblical reflection is to identify the primary issues around which the authentic biblical story of God's action in the world is centred and to present them with confidence and clarity.

This was an important factor in the Alliance's decision to develop a theological commission. The Alliance's Commission on Unity and Truth among Evangelicals (ACUTE) launched in 1994 came about as a pan-evangelical response to theological issues which could effect unity among evangelicals. ACUTE came on the scene at an important time, for 1994 was to be a year in which British evangelicals found themselves facing a number of tensions. It was the year in which Christians in Britain were presented with four UK-wide evangelistic initiatives. The Churches Together in Britain and Ireland presented evangelistic opportunities around Lent, Steve Chalke's 'On Fire' opened up creative ideas for community-orientated evangelism, while the German evangelist Reinhard Bonke's organisation Christ for the Nations promised to get an evangelistic booklet into every home. Significantly, Pentecostals in

Britain came together to launch 'JIM', a major evangelistic campaign which worked to include all the major Black and White Pentecostal groups in Britain. 'JIM' (Jesus in Me) was a radical departure from Pentecostal individualism which also brought its own challenges for relationships between Black and White Pentecostals as much as Pentecostal relationships within the wider evangelical Church.

By the summer months we were faced with serious discussions about the American evangelist, Morris Cerullo. The problem was that his annual London-wide Mission to London was a member of the Evangelical Alliance and was attracting high-profile controversy as a result of his emphasis on miracles, fund-raising strategies and his classical Pentecostal cultural approach to evangelism.

But the summer of 1994 was sizzling with other controversies. A new phenomenon labelled the 'Toronto Blessing' was beginning to take Britain by storm. Its roots were traceable back to the ministries of Latin-American Pentecostal leaders but at the epicentre of the phenomenon was a young South African evangelist, Rodney Brown, whose holy laughter-dispensing ministry had profoundly affected a small, hitherto unknown church situated below the flight path of Toronto Airport. The small congregation, which was then linked to John Wimber's Vineyard ministry, found itself at the centre of a world-wide pilgrimage for a new phenomenon which expressed itself in unusual acts of laughter or remorse and became typified by a range of physical responses. In May, the phenomenon made its identifiable debut on the British scene during an afternoon leaders' reception where Eleanor Mumford, a leader with the Vineyard church in Britain, was recounting her experiences in Toronto to church leaders at Holy Trinity Brompton in Knightsbridge, London. Within a short period the Toronto Blessing was both pervasive and sought-after in church life. It was also to become the most controversial development within British church life for many decades, producing almost as many books and articles as it did converts! In December I was invited to facilitate a special meeting of senior evangelical leaders across the divide to discuss the phenomenon. It was to be the first of three forums which the Alliance provided for its members and friends to discuss our differing views and was a central pool from which discussions in Northern Ireland, Scotland and Wales all took place.

The 'Toronto' debates were important to British evangelicalism. They were fundamentally about the presuppositions from which we approach biblical truth as much as our genuine commitment to the truth which was so evidently a concern of all those who participated in the debates. There were notable exceptions, but the general rule was that Pentecostals and charismatics had fewer difficulties with the phenomenon. Everyone insisted that the Bible was important in the debate, but it soon became evident that while conservative evangelicals read the Bible for clear biblical consent with which to allow the unusual, those who were less critical read the Bible to identify a lack of prohibitions which gave scope for the unusual. Some thought it was demonic and others were quite convinced that it was a precursor to revival. Not everyone understood that as an Alliance our responsibility was to guide our members through the important theological points of the debate, encouraging good pastoral practice and ensuring that we expressed our differences in a spirit of humility.

Towards the end of that year other issues began to loom large. Anglicans were being torn in different directions over such matters as the ordination of women, debates on sexuality and the emergence of a distinctly evangelical group called Reform. The Anglican Leaders' Conference of January 1995 was over-subscribed and therefore took place in Westminster Chapel. Very little was made of this irony during the conference but I could not help reflecting on the fact that this Chapel had the greatest reputation for evangelical independence in the United Kingdom, for it was here at Westminster Chapel, during a meeting of the Evangelical Alliance in 1966, that Dr Martyn Lloyd-Jones made a dramatic appeal for evangelicals to 'come out' from the compromise of the broad Church and was openly rebutted by the chairman of the conference, John Stott. The episode was very damaging to evangelical relationships. As I sat watching senior evangelical Anglicans standing in the very place in which 'the Doctor' ministered over many years, I couldn't help wondering what he would have made of the event.

A number of contributions stood out in my mind. Quite apart from the Anglican dilemma of whether we have a 'Church of England' or the 'Church for England', I was particularly struck by Dick France's outstanding presentation on Jesus' inclusive ministry drawn from a comparison between Mark 9:38–41 and Matthew 12:30. Equally important to the conference was Michael Baughan's appeal for 'grace and truth' to coexist.

All of these were vital if isolated examples of the struggles for identity and meaning which helped to consolidate my own convictions about evangelical diversity. These important scraps of experiences meant a great deal to me as the local pastor of a growing church made up of young adults who themselves had to work out what it meant to be authentically Black Christians who took the Bible seriously. My multiple experiences made it harder for me to be as dogmatic about issues which once were of major importance. Even more than ever, I was unconvinced that there was anything to be gained by excessive emphasis on the minutia of our denominational codes about jewellery and hat-wearing. Some of my theological convictions also came under closer scrutiny. I certainly remained convinced about the fact of Christ's return and its significance for us, in terms of both our ethical behaviour and our final account-ability. But I became less convinced about the dogmatism of a pre-millennium Second Coming which appeared to raise as many questions as it answered. Such an interpre-tation of the books of Daniel and Revelation became an unnecessary test of orthodoxy about a theological position which will only become finally knowable in the future.

I also became uncomfortable about the over-emphasis on tongues as the initial evidence of the baptism of the Holy Spirit. Few people in my congregation would have understood the significance of sermons which replaced the 'initial evidence' emphasis with a 'substantial evidence' emphasis. I still believed that many people spoke in known or unknown languages as a direct result of the work of God's Spirit. In fact I remained convinced that this unusual gift which was so evident in the early Church was a valid measurement of what the New Testament described as the 'baptism of the Holy Spirit'. My real concern was with the tendency to elevate this phenomenon above other expressions of the Spirit's work in the life of the believer and to make it a mark of distinction rather than a natural part of what God does in the life of a believer. I became equally concerned about the 'substantial evidence' of the baptism of the Holy Spirit showing itself in spiritual maturity, personal holiness and a greater range of spiritual gifts which were all too often marginalised by the over-emphasis on one particular gift.

Increasingly it seemed that a wider theological lens did not require a denial of my essential Pentecostal position if I happened to challenge what appeared to be secondary issues. Within my own denomination I continued to walk a precarious path between total involvement as a member of the National Executive Council to which I was appointed in 1992, the work of a local pastorate which did not reflect the denominational consensus in all its details, and the wider work as the UK Director of the Evangelical Alliance. Much of the demands of local ministry were shared by a pastoral team – in itself a radical departure for our denomination – and an assistant who provided pastoral leadership during my absence. The benefits of this wider involvement for the church, myself and my family were gradually being outweighed by the physical demands of trying to be in too many places at the same time.

The whole thing came to head on the pavement outside the church after a Sunday evening service. I was talking to a critical young man who specialised in pulling things apart. He was particularly critical of the fact that I was increasingly away from the church and made it clear that he thought having two major responsibilities was irresponsible. In fact what this young man did was to trigger in me a growing conviction that it was impossible to do both things effectively. But it was more than that. It was the old restlessness again. I began to realise that it was time to leave the local church. It was a particularly difficult thing to acknowledge given that the church had recently committed itself to becoming far more conscious about being a discipling centre, was experiencing steady growth and was about to move location to a larger building.

I became aware that I would leave the local church during a leadership retreat in the spring of 1995. My main responsibility was to kick-start the weekend designed to reshape our church, drawing up a mission statement and a new teaching programme for the year. It was actually as I watched the leadership at work reshaping and dreaming about a new direction that I became convinced that I would no longer be in the forefront of its leadership.

Sunday 15 October was a strange day. It was my birthday and in the morning worship I was given a surprise gift by the congregation. In the evening service I announced that I would be leaving! Within a few weeks the congregation, under the direction of our national office, invited my assistant to become the new pastor. The church conference took place on a Wednesday evening in November. The following day, without realising what had taken place the night before, the Alliance, refocusing on its senior management, asked me to assume a new responsibility of 'team leader' within the senior management team. Effectively, this involved a co-ordinating role within the Alliance's leadership integrating the teams and providing the space for Clive as the Director General to pursue the wider task of working with media and press. It was also a recognition of the role I was asked to play as the chair for the forthcoming Assembly the following November.

The year 1996 was to be one of celebration for the Alliance. It was 150 years since its beginning in 1846, and this was to be marked by a series of celebrations throughout the UK. Celebrations were held in Scotland, Wales and Northern Ireland as well as Manchester and Wembley. As a tribute to Gilbert Kirby, a former General Secretary of the Alliance, an edited publication, *For Such a Time as This*, was produced. The highpoint of the year was a National Assembly held in Bournemouth from 11 to 13 November, attended by nearly 3,000 church leaders and members of the Alliance.

We approached the Assembly with a combination of concern and excitement. It was the first formal Assembly since the difficult meeting in 1966 when John Stott had challenged Martyn Lloyd-Jones over his appeal for evangelicals to leave the compromise of the broad Church. We were aware of similar, growing tensions within evangelicalism. Not only were there underlying questions about spirituality, characterised by the Toronto debates, the debate about evangelical identity was now being underlined by discussions about 'post-evangelicalism' raised by the former House Church leader, David Tomlinson.

The Assembly was the first public test of the strength of our unity for thirty years. A combination of main platform addresses, worship and twelve seminar streams helped us reflect on the context of our post-modern world, review the nature of our own evangelical diversity and raise important questions about how we engaged with society. It was a privilege to serve such an event which provided a forum for British evangelicals to ask tentative and important questions. In one sense it was also a 'safe setting' in which we were able to agree that we were not all the same but that there were common issues which held us together. The things we agreed together in the closing moments of the Assembly were affirmed in what we called 'The Bournemouth Declaration'.

The Bournemouth Declaration – An Evangelical Agenda

We, the National Assembly of Evangelicals, meeting in Bournemouth, November 11–13 1996, rejoice in God's grace and patience, conscious of the privileges we enjoy. We have listened to God and each other and present this agenda as a reflection of our discussion together.

Christ, Scripture and Unity

We honour Jesus Christ alone as Saviour and Lord. His atoning death, bodily resurrection and personal return are central to Christian faith.

We resolve to proclaim to all the reality of new life through the Cross.

We confess the Lord Jesus Christ as God's Word incarnate; supreme authority is His. We recognise Scripture as God's

Word written, the definitive, normative and sufficient revelation of God's truth.

We repent of our neglect of Scripture and resolve to study, live and apply it relevantly in our world.

We recognise that unity is both God's gift and God's intention for His people. He has made us one in Christ; He wants us to express that invisible one-ness in visible ways. We believe that unity becomes visible primarily through our shared commitment to God's Word, to each other and to His work.

We acknowledge our failure to maintain the unity of the Spirit.

Our one-ness in Christ requires us to work together with integrity:

- to attempt to distinguish primary from secondary issues and to clarify the extent to which differing terminology can properly express the same truth;
- to affirm diversity and reach mutual understanding on secondary issues;
- to treat each other with love and grace and to live by the spirit of the 1846 Evangelical Alliance's 'Practical Resolutions'.

Church and Mission

Mission begins with God, who calls us to share in reaching the world with His redeeming love. As Christ was sent by the Father, He now sends us in the power of the Holy Spirit. We recommit ourselves to this mission with renewed confidence in the one God revealed uniquely in Christ, and in the one gospel to be proclaimed to all people. We believe the Church is the community of faith which is called to be an authentic expression of the gospel and a sign of the Kingdom of God by:

- developing missionary congregations of all ages, reaching across social, linguistic and geographical boundaries;
- planting radical and creative churches in unreached communities and people groups;
- releasing the vision, zeal and skills of younger leaders;
- recognising cultural diversity as part of our life and witness in the world;
- seeking to engage with the increasing pluralism of our world;
- rethinking the way we communicate and model gospel truth, love and reconciliation;
- receiving from and giving to the world-wide Christian family;
- preparing for future challenges and opportunities.

Church and Society

God created and sustains the world, and has given His human creatures stewardship over all He has made. We recognise that no area of life is outside God's sovereign rule. We take the incarnation and transforming work of Christ as our model for engagement. We affirm our commitment to releasing Christian people for involvement at all levels of society, informed by Scripture and enabled by the Holy Spirit.

We believe it is important for the Church to be a listening people.

We acknowledge our common humanity, rooted in the image of God, and our shared responsibility to:

- uphold and defend the sanctity of human life, and protect and promote all that contributes to human dignity and development;
- build and maintain peace and reconciliation between

communities and peoples in conflict;

- pursue justice and compassion within our society and the wider world;
- promote teaching and training for responsible family living;
- oppose all forms of racism in Church and society;
- resist the tendency to marginalise others, and act to break down barriers of prejudice;
- promote a positive expression of sexuality, in singleness and marriage, freeing everyone to develop the rich variety of friendships God intended, as revealed in Scripture.

Conclusion

Recognising our total dependence upon God, we commit ourselves to pray and work together to equip and mobilise Christians of all ages in pursuit of this agenda.

We repent of our past failures, and pray for reformation and renewal in the Church and for a spiritual awakening throughout these islands.

6

Reasons to be Cheerful

There was a genuine up-beat optimism about as thousands of Christians gathered to march to Hyde Park. The banners, exuberance and fanfare environment said it all. March for Jesus! Whatever you made of the idea of marching on the streets as a mark of Christian witness, it was difficult to take away the sense of significance which accompanied the 1994 March for Jesus, with over 75,000 committed Christians proclaiming Christ as they streamed endlessly into Hyde Park. The event was an amazing story of success which started tentatively in 1987 when just over 15,000 Christians marched through the City of London in the pouring rain.

The outdoor celebration itself was an array of high-profile Christian leaders flanked by a wide spectrum of enthusiastic Christians, beaming, worshipping and brandishing banners under an open blue sky. March for Jesus had come to be regarded as another important expression of confident non-partisan Christian witness which stood in cheerful defiance of declining Christian witness. During the open air service in Hyde Park I was introduced to a special American visitor. Under his broad-brimmed hat he sported a keen face with a ready smile and attentive eyes. His slender frame came with a positive and firm handshake. His name was Tom Sine. Tom, the author of a number of celebrated books including *Wild Hope*, described himself as a biblical futurologist. He is known to have a keen interest in global patterns and the impact of social and demographic trends on the life of the Church.

It soon became clear that Tom was very impressed by British evangelicalism and relationships across the Christian community in the United Kingdom. Frankly, so much of my work had engulfed me in discussions about fragmentation and signs of divisions that I had given little attention to anything positive about Christian relationships in Britain. Tom Sine was full of praise. March for Jesus itself stood out in his own mind as a clear indication of the advantage which British Christians had in positive working relationships. A similar venture was hard to envisage in the United States. Indeed he was sufficiently impressed by evangelical diversity and the work of the Evangelical Alliance that he dedicated his next book, *Cease Fire*, to 'my friends in the Evangelical Alliance in Great Britain'. It seemed that there were things to celebrate if we took the time to reflect on developments around us.

In many ways it could be said that the 1980s and 1990s have been good years for evangelicalism. Certainly, within the international setting, evangelical faith has experienced significant growth. The World Evangelical Fellowship, spanning 120 countries, represented over 300 million Christians world-wide. A Gallup poll 1978–9 estimated between 40 and 50 million evangelicals in the United States with rising interest in Christian books and conferences.

Much of the growth in the international Church appeared to be generated through charismatic/Pentecostal groups, which accounted for 80 per cent of Christian converts world-wide. In Africa, Asia and Latin America, people were being converted more quickly than they could be discipled. South Korea, with only one Christian church at the turn of the century, now had a 30 per cent Christian population. Some very important lessons were being held up around us as we came to realise that the balance of influence in the world Church was slowly shifting from the north to the south of the equator. In 1993 London Bible College invited a fellow student, the Ghanaian theologian Kwame Bediako, to deliver the annual Laing Lecture. His address, 'Cry Jesus', drew from his own context as an African church leader and theologian. Kwame pointed out that the international Christian witness was 53 per cent non-White and that perhaps for the first time in its history Christianity could truly claim to be an international religion. Increasingly it occurred to me that the international Christian community was composed of two groups: those who were creating statistics and those of us who were counting them.

Not surprisingly, Britain was also experiencing the overflow of this international development. The 1989 English Church Census showed that of the 3.9 million Christians attending church each week, one million of them were evangelicals. Forty-seven per cent of Christians were charismatic/Pentecostals. This steady growth of charismatic and Pentecostal evangelicalism was a factor in the growth and profile of evangelicals in Britain. Events such as Spring Harvest and March for Jesus were important symbols of this new, confident profile, which has contributed to the popular view that 'charismatic' is a synonym for 'evangelical'. Easter People, the Methodist charismatic conference which began in 1988 with 1,000 people, had leapt to 12,000 guests from a wide range of church streams beyond Methodism in 1998. In other parts of the evangelical Church, the Fellowship of Independent Evangelical Churches (FIEC) spoke of steady growth in their 1998 Caister conference and the Proclamation Trust's annual Assembly has hosted a growing number of delegates each year. Both the FIEC, which provides support and fellowship for independent churches throughout Britain, and the Proclamation Trust, which has a special focus on promoting expository preaching, would not be typified by charismatic worship and preaching, although both have small numbers of Pentecostal and charismatic churches in their membership.

Alongside these events, the important work of evangelical ministries such as Christian Action Research and Education (CARE), Tearfund's overseas relief work and ACET's powerful response to Aids and HIV-positive victims, made it clear that evangelicals were prepared to become involved in the real world.

Evangelical Christian faith increasingly became a significant feature of church life across the denominations with growing numbers of Anglican ordinands claiming to be evangelicals. In 1990 the entire Christian community was surprised by the appointment of the evangelical Bishop of Bath and Wells, Dr George Carey, as the new Archbishop of Canterbury. The Archbishop's Decade of Evangelism was inaugurated shortly after he took up office, and since then the Alpha friendship evangelism programme has raised the profile of church-based evangelism, having a rapid impact on thousands of churches across the UK, America, Australia and many other parts of the world.

Along with other groups, the Evangelical Alliance was an integral part of this period of development. By the time I had been appointed UK Director in 1992, the Alliance had increased its membership by 25 per cent each year over a period of five years. By 1995 the Alliance's membership held together over 600 societies and 3,000 local churches in 25 organisational groups and denominations with a constituency of a million Christians. Between 1980 and 1995 EA's Council grew from twenty to seventy-five in order to reflect the diversity of its growing membership.

During this important period of evangelical expansionism much was done to regain credibility. Evangelicals had come a long way from the days when Hensley Henson, a former Bishop of Durham, described them as 'an army of illiterates, generalled by octogenarians . . . inclined to the view that they are excused culture, scholarship and intellectual exercise on religious grounds'. From the 1950s much work had been done to sow the seeds of credible scholarship through the work of prominent scholars and teachers such as Stott, Packer, Schaeffer and Carl Henry in the United States. Contemporary evangelicalism has benefited from the work of organisations such as Universities and Colleges Christian Fellowship, Rutherford House, and Bible institutes such as London Bible College and the Evangelical Theological College in Wales.

A leading column in *The Sunday Times Magazine* of 16 December 1990 summarised the period aptly. 'Whatever you may think of them . . . tomorrow belongs to the evangelicals.' Such a statement from a secular paper was no indication that the battle against unhelpful caricatures had been fought and won, but it did suggest that evangelicalism had earned the right to be taken more seriously, not least because an increasing number of evangelicals like Clive Calver, Elaine Storkey of Christian Impact, David Holloway, Vicar of Jesmond, David Cook of the Whitefield Institute and Steve Chalke of the Oasis Trust, became media-friendly, presenting clear biblical values.

In this ferment of optimism many of my own thoughts about Christian unity in diversity were being realised. It wasn't that all was well with the evangelical world, it was simply that all was not bad. The growth which was taking place around us meant that the world in which I ministered had become an intersection of ideas and relationships and activity. What was even more fascinating was that I found myself meandering between the 'tribes' of evangelicalism, learning and absorbing their varied shapes and cultures as an integral part of what I was doing. My ability to do so was due in part to the tireless effort which many key church leaders had put into developing a diverse community which enjoyed a measure of mutual trust. But there were other factors at work which made it possible for so much mutuality to emerge in the evangelical Church.

In the first place, the British Church is relatively small in comparison with our American cousins or the wider expanse of European Christianity. Added to this, the south-east focus of the Christian world, which is so often a source of despair for people in Scotland, Northern Ireland, Wales and other parts of England, has to some extent meant that the same faces have appeared wearing different hats in numerous committees with different names. In a totally practical way, geography and transport have thrown disparate people together. Compared with the rambling vastness of America or Asia, and the cultural and linguistic diversity in Europe, Britain is a relatively homogenous place with real but often invisible boundaries of tradition and compatible culture. In Britain, the word 'nation' is often sensitive, but we are unlikely to come to blows over its misuse on public platforms.

Over the past twenty years we have also benefited from a growing number of cross-conferences, importing guest speakers from neighbouring traditions. For two years, Elim and the Assemblies of God amalgamated their annual conferences and have increasingly held joint meetings of their executives with invitations to a wider fraternity of Pentecostals. The renewed fellowship of Pentecostals gained impetus with JIM, the Pentecostal evangelistic initiative in 1994, and resulted in the formation of the Pentecostal Churches of the UK in 1997 with Wynne Lewis, Superintendent of Elim, as its chair and Io Smith, the Black female church leader from the New Testament Assembly, as its vice-chair.

The plethora of publications available to Christian leaders and the wider Christian public has provided a pan-denominational notice-board introducing church members to names and activities beyond their own groups and streams. In fact the desire to keep up with the flourishing demand for this emerging, inter-church mind-set has meant that denominational publications have increasingly reflected the activities of a wider community.

Undoubtedly, our label-free culture has had a direct impact on our attitudes to church loyalty which has resulted not only in a wider pan-denominational approach to church life but also to a post-denominational understanding of church. Derek Tidball, Principal of London Bible College, for many years a leading pan-evangelical college, has identified 'a discernible trend' in denominational ambiguity in recent years. Even when they have identified themselves within a congregational setting, very few Christians appear to have a real grasp of a congregational theology.

Clive Calver told the story of a radio interview with the former Conservative cabinet minister, Kenneth Clarke. The minister was totally confused about evangelical politics, unable to determine whether it was to the right, left or centre of the political spectrum. He was bemused to learn that it was reflected in all three. This lack of political polarisation in British Christianity is something we may be very grateful for. British Christianity has certainly benefited from a culture of political tolerance and has moved a long way from the days when Christianity could be summarised as the Conservative Party at prayer.

The philosopher Voltaire once remarked, 'If a thing is too foolish to say, it can always be sung.' True enough; and who would want to argue with Voltaire on this particular issue having heard some of the more contemporary ditties in the modern Church? But I have no doubt that the most unifying influence of all has been the rise of new all-church songs which have poured from the pens of modern hymnodists, song writers and worship leaders. During my travels it soon became evident that the power of the sung word was probably greater than the power of the spoken word in bringing Christians together. Not all songs have met with universal approval in all places but from the classic hymns of the eighteenth and nineteenth centuries and the works of Timothy Dudley-Smith and Michael Saward to Graham Kendrick, Noel Richards and Matt Redman, the Christian Church has come to drink deeply at the same fountains of inspiration – irrespective of our theological differences.

I became acutely aware of this during my second visit to the Keswick Convention, as we happily sang a Dave Fellingham song knowing that it was unlikely that Dave would lead from its platform in the foreseeable future. In fact when I saw Dave a few weeks later at the New Frontiers conference in Stoneleigh and told him how much I enjoyed his song at Keswick, he laughed hysterically. It so happened that he was visiting a friend within earshot of the Convention and heard it on his way past.

What has been equally unifying about worship in recent years has been the return to the historic anchorage of the old hymns in the creativity of the new. I attended a large charismatic gathering in Bristol in which there was an ample supply of the energetic decibel worship with which we have become familiar. Without pre-empting it, the worship leader led us into an old hymn: 'My Jesus, I love Thee, I know Thou art mine . . .' It was tangibly unifying. Delegates at the second DAWN (Discipling A Whole Nation) Congress in Nottingham in 1995 experienced a similar resonance when Graham Kendrick led the conference in an old Salvationist song, 'Send the fire!' And who can close their heart or mind to the plaintive tones of 'Here is love'?

Music has always been that 'food of love' by which God draws us closer to Himself and invariably to each other. It is little wonder that Christians of all persuasions gravitate towards the Psalms, which happen to be songs of the soul.

Through the gift of worship and our increased ability to communicate across our historic boundaries, God has gradually given us insights into our corporateness even when we sing and worship apart.

We shouldn't underrate the importance of prayer in all of this. The fact is that over the last twenty years prayer movements, prayer triplets, neighbourhood prayer watches and prayer walks have forged cross-denominational relationships through local, national and international movements. Prayer for Revival in Birmingham and March for Jesus are just two outstanding examples worth citing. The growing 'ecumenism of the Spirit' is a close relative of the prayer movement, pulling together as it has a wide spectrum of theological distinctives around the growing phenomenon of charismatic experience. The Charismatic Leaders' Conference, which meets by invitation at the beginning of each year, has been the most constant expression of this charismatic meeting place which goes wider than the evangelical Church, bound together by the common denominator of a Trinitarian confession and a charismatic/Pentecostal experience. This group, composed primarily of senior leaders with nation-wide responsibilities, provides a combination of fellowship, theological reflection and prayer and has grown steadily in its range and size over the past five years.

Perhaps the last unifying influence to add is the tendency towards social action which pulls Christians together in practical deeds on behalf of the community. It is what Francis Schaeffer described as 'co-belligerence' and describes the strategy of working for the common good irrespective of theological distinctives. Indeed, co-belligerence may even be extended to non-Christians who share similar values and whose partnership for practical purposes would not compromise Christian faith. Needless to say, not all evangelicals would subscribe to these aspects of 'unity'. There is always a path to be forged between abject separatism and confusing compromise.

But despite the brisk breezes of controversies and tensions which quickly became a feature of my new role in 1992, I also learned to reflect on and appreciate my stroll along the countryside of evangelical diversity. In 1993 I visited the Keswick Convention in Cumbria for the first time. As a preacher who loved preaching I was first attracted to the event when I learned of its long-standing and prestigious history as the oldest preaching conference in the world. But it was its well-known theme 'All One In Christ' which first attracted my attention. When I suggested to a friend that I would love to attend the conference he thought it was a rather amusing idea. It was his impression that the Convention, as well as the theme, was somewhat conservative. He seemed to think that a Black Pentecostal leader linked to the Evangelical Alliance would be something of a misfit at Keswick. My first move was to visit Philip Hacking, Vicar of Christchurch Fullwood in Sheffield then chair of the Convention. Our time together was very positive and led me to anticipate my first visit to Keswick even more than I did before.

That first two-day visit in 1993 was very memorable. The Cumbrian scenery was an attraction on its own but I was also glad to see my friend and former LBC colleague Alistair Begg whom I had not seen since graduation. It was only during his second sermon on Daniel that I realised I had never heard him preach despite spending three years together at Bible college.

Keswick was old, historic and quaint but I loved it. Much of the customs and table-talk were salutations to its history and its pride of place in the tradition of expository preaching. The old names of Redpath, Leith Samuel and Rhyle were a part of its esoteric past. It appeared to be indifferent to contemporary culture and yet it held a deep fascination for me. It was as though the deposits of many years of faithful proclamation of the Gospel refused to be marginalised by the passage of time.

There were genuine attempts to ensure that I was 'OK' given that this was not my 'usual scene'. It certainly was not a New Testament Church of God Convention or even a Spring Harvest, and I found myself deeply grateful that it was not. It had a life and character of its own. And beneath the canopy of the famous tent with its sleepy old women for whom Keswick had become an unbreakable habit, the neatly packaged services, tentative drum rolls and precision communion service, was a deep and abiding commitment to the Bible. I felt strangely at home. Over lunch I suggested that my emotional proximity to Keswick probably had a lot to do with the deep streams of holiness preaching, which were such an integral part of its theological position and history, and which had had such a profound impact on my own holiness tradition as a classical Pentecostal.

My first visit to Keswick was brief but it was long enough to know that I would find some reason to return – not just because I had been so helped by the commitment to the Bible but also because I felt a growing commitment to change as it became aware of contemporary culture. I was quite surprised and humbled by the invitation, which followed a few months later, to join its council.

It was becoming clear that God was working to bring streams together, and much of the work I was becoming involved with gave me the privilege of being a first-hand witness to God's strategic work of repairing broken links and breaking down walls.

I had heard a great deal about Bryn Jones and his work with Covenant Ministries. We first met in 1992 for a series of planning meetings and I was very pleased to be invited to a regional leaders' meeting at their headquarters in Nettlehill in October 1993. Most of us would have been aware of the somewhat detached relationship with the main streams of evangelicalism which Covenant Ministries had had up to that point and the deep tracks of separateness between charismatic groups highlighted in Andrew Walker's *Restoring the Kingdom*. It just so happened that my visit was the first of a series of visits from separated brethren which was to follow. It was a quantum leap of courage and determination to fix the future.

In the same period I was reunited with another former friend and colleague. I picked up a news item about Terry Virgo leaving the UK to minister in the United States. In the meanwhile, the article ran, the UK work of New Frontiers International was to be co-ordinated by Terry's colleague, David Holden. I had not seen David since graduation and wrote to congratulate him in the hope that he would remember who I was. In fact David not only remembered that we knew each other but reminded me of aspects of our time together at LBC which I had forgotten about! He recalled, for example, the fact that we spent a year together in the same placement taking the Sunday School at the little Methodist church in Ruislip. Our reminiscing over lunch led to a meeting with the London NFI leaders in November 1993 and my first visit to the Stoneleigh international conference in 1994. It was a very impressive gathering of some 20,000 charismatic Christians which has experienced rapid growth since its beginning in 1991. At that meeting there were 8,000 people. By my third visit in 1996, there were 20,000 visitors over two weeks, of whom over 20 per cent were visitors beyond the NFI community.

Perhaps more than anything else, this meeting of the evangelical streams has been a source of encouragement to our work of reconciliation, and I have been both buffeted and blessed by the demands of this development. It has shown itself in a variety of ways in recent years and should,

I believe, give us some reasons to be thankful.

Much of this evangelical mingling has been about the development of personal relationships. Between 1993 and 1995 London enjoyed the impact of London for Jesus, amounting to key meetings in the capital resulting from a growing relationship between five key leaders. The combination of Sandy Millar, the senior leader of Holy Trinity Brompton, Gerald Coates of Pioneer, Roger Forster from Ichthus, Lynn Green, the European Director of Youth with a Mission, and Colin Dye, the senior pastor of Kensington Temple, the largest church in Europe, was a very powerful statement about the strength of growing relationships in the interest of common goals.

From 1988 the Apostolic Team Leaders from several of the New Churches had been meeting to repair old broken bridges, pray and think together about common concerns. Their decision to disclose their meetings to the Christian public with a press release in 1998 took many people by surprise, given the diversity of personalities in the group. Similarly, many of us were pleasantly surprised by the inclusion of Gerald Coates as a special guest at Selwyn Hughes' seventieth birthday celebrations at CWR (Crusade for World Revival) Waverley Abbey.

Also in 1998, a group of conservative evangelicals introduced Essential Evangelicals, an informal forum for 'gospel' people who believe that much of mainstream evangelicalism is in danger of losing some of the distinctive features of Reformation theology in preaching, teaching and application. The commitment of Essential Evangelicals is to reinforce the Reformation principles which are integral to historic evangelicalism, without becoming a separatist movement.

Evangelicals cannot afford to practise togetherness at the expense of biblical integrity. The tension between unity and truth has ever been an important issue for people who wish to take the Bible seriously. Increasingly, my work forced me to examine not only what I thought I saw on the complex and exciting Christian landscape; it also forced me time and again to examine the lens through which I viewed the world beyond myself. I was not alone. The hermeneutical debate was on.

Hermeneutics is the study of the principles which guide our interpretation and understanding of Scriptures. I recall a conversation with an eminent evangelical leader in which I raised the question of hermeneutics. He was not impressed. In fact he suggested that hermeneutics was only a complicated word which Christians used to make the Bible say whatever they want! It was a sobering thought for although I did not agree with his cavalier dismissiveness I could see that this could so easily be the case. Dave Tomlinson, the former House Church leader, emerged from London Bible College's Master's degree in hermeneutics to engage us in a vigorous debate about post-evangelicalism – a debate which is unlikely to go away in the near future. Tomlinson has raised important questions about the historic framework within which evangelicals have approached theology. His underlying concern has been that the evangelicalism shaped by the Reformers has produced an outdated set of responses for many thinking evangelicals working out their faith in a complex society. His views and conclusions, which appear to court a liberal biblical and moral position, are unlikely to convince significant numbers of church leaders, but it is true to say that many of the questions he has raised resonate for a growing number of young evangelical Christians.

What has been rewarding, however, is the extent to which the various streams of church life have been willing to engage in the theological discovery together. The willingness to hear and be heard is an important development which British evangelicals have begun to explore more earnestly. I was intrigued to learn from my colleague, Arfon Jones, General Secretary of the Evangelical Alliance in Wales, that in the two expository preaching seminars hosted by the Alliance in 1992 and 1993 the majority of those who attended to hear David Jackman from the Proclamation Trust were Pentecostal and charismatic leaders. In fact, the influential Cornhill teaching programme, regarded as a leading training tool for expository preaching in the conservative evangelical mould, has seen a steady influx of Pentecostal and charismatic students.

When the Toronto phenomenon arrived in the UK, it was particularly gratifying that senior church leaders were prepared to spend many hours in different forums discussing an event which few of us truly understood and about which we had very different points of view. As I mentioned in the previous chapter this was a particularly important development for the evangelical Church and possibly taught us as much about the need to work together with our differences as anything else. In the first of our three key leaders' meetings discussing the events of this period, I chatted through the implications of what we were doing with the late Professor Tudor Jones. Professor Jones, an eminent Welsh historian with a specialism in revival history, was a very godly and irenic man. I asked him if he knew of a comparable event when church leaders met, as we were doing, to talk together from different perspectives in the face of an unusual and controversial phenomenon. He couldn't think of one. It was this kind of pulling together, along with the numerous public debates throughout the United Kingdom, which gave me hope for our capacity to work together and which made sense of how people like Tom Sine saw evangelical witness in Britain.

Slowly but surely, the old dichotomy between an unthinking emotionalism and cerebral Christianity devoid of power is being undermined by a new exploration into the relationship between the Word and Spirit. Modern evangelicalism owes much to the work, study and passion of men like the late Bob Gordon, Roy Clements and R.T. Kendall for these truths helping us reconcile the power of the Spirit and the authority of the Word. The dichotomy is no longer safe as we are increasingly exposed to the clear theological minds of scholars whose theological insights and charismatic experience will continue to challenge us to think biblically as we experience God.

When in 1994 the Alliance decided to set up its Theological Commission, I became responsible to set it in motion. The thinking was that this body would undergird the Alliance's work with clear theological reflection for its activities and would identify issues which could potentially divide us. There was a clear rationale to do theology relationally and from a broad evangelical spectrum.

ACUTE – the Alliance Commission on Unity and Truth among Evangelicals – got off the ground with vital input from Dave Cave, a church leader and urban theologian from Liverpool who did an excellent task in setting up the infrastructure. It was not easy to set up as it needed the right balance of the constituency, a good mix of theological expertise and practitioners. The steering group was also flanked by specialists available beyond the steering group meetings. Its membership ranged from members of the British Evangelical Council and the Evangelical Movement of Wales to charismatic and Pentecostal theologians.

Its first significant piece of work, prepared in time for the 1996 Assembly, explored the issue of evangelical identity in *What is an Evangelical?* The booklet did not attempt to be an exhaustive treatment of this very difficult question but rather to raise questions about the attitudes and biblical principles necessary in addressing the issue. Its later works reflected on the Toronto meetings, human sexuality, prosperity and heaven and hell: all attempts to grapple with complex and difficult questions with honesty and biblical integrity.

The Commission and the work of EA's theological secretary, David Hilborn, has been an important statement of intent. It is the acknowledgment that theology is important and must remain important to credible biblical witness. But it is also a realisation that the work of biblical reflection cannot and should not be done in isolated theological compartments.

There are good reasons to be grateful and British Christians need to spend time reflecting on how much we have to be thankful for. There is a pessimism which is endemic in the British psyche and which has etched its way into the Christian mindset by which all things good come up for cynical scrutiny. Success and prosperity are exclusively American Christian ideas which have no legitimacy in British Christian experience; we are happiest when we are unhappy. But there are reasons to be cheerful and we should spend time reflecting on them.

7

Reasons to be Careful

I pushed the door to Broadcasting House with a combination of elation and apprehension. It is the kind of nervous tension which accompanies most of us before a significant performance and, on this occasion, I was particularly anxious about my impending interview. It was Sunday, 8 June 1997, and I was about to be interviewed for BBC Radio 4's *Sunday* programme following my appointment as EA's General Director. It was the culmination of a long process which seemed to have lasted for ever. I had spent eight days in meetings and briefings, with a press conference at Church House the previous Friday. Both the national and Christian press had been very generous with their coverage of the story. It seemed as if the brief interview I was about to have would be the final, formal declaration of the 'thing' which the evangelical Church had done to me.

In effect, the journey had lasted for the better part of a year. As EA's UK Director I became a team leader for the senior management group. Clive Calver's decision in the spring to accept the appointment as President of the American evangelical relief agency, World Relief, created a flurry of activity at the Alliance. The job was rightly and wisely advertised – despite the fact that so many friends assumed my role to be a natural stepping-stone to the job. It was a difficult in-between time. Frankly, I was very reticent about entering the interview process but felt it was right to do so. I received a great deal of kindness, support and encouragement as I thought very deeply about the implications for myself, my family and the Alliance. It was also a very important time to reflect on all that God had been doing in my life over the years. To some extent, I felt like a man who had been strapped into a chair slowly moving through the years of my life.

The first interview took place on 1 May, the day of the general election which put Tony Blair and the Labour Party into government. That was followed by a second interview with the selection panel on 28 May shortly after the international conference of the World Evangelical Fellowship in Abbottsford, Vancouver. The formal announcement meant that I began my new role on 1 June.

The BBC interview was over very quickly and it was not particularly harrowing. How did I feel about being the first Black director in the Alliance's 150-year history? I suggested that, just as my predecessor's appointment had been a vote of confidence for radical youth fourteen years previously, so I saw my appointment as a vote of confidence for evangelical diversity. Other questions followed, but the one piercing question which stayed with me all day showed that the interviewer had done some homework. He asked: given that we represented a million evangelicals dealing with such a wide range of opinions and issues, how did we hope to keep everyone together? Wasn't this going to be an impossible task?

The story of British Christianity is the tale of two cities. On the one hand there is a great deal for which we must be thankful; at the same time there are ominous signs on the horizon. The irony is that both stand in creative tension, for invariably the very things which make us strong as a community of faith are the things which could pull us apart.

British evangelicalism has been a cyclical story of strong

and clear witness under duress and of fragmentation when we have become larger and confident. In many ways, the odds are stacked heavily against our staying firm together. Our ability to enter the next millennium with a strident and coherent witness will be sorely tested.

In the first place we all struggle with the fragmentation of a contemporary culture which has very little loyalty to history or institutions. In a society where communities have become fragmented, where more and more people belong to single-parent homes and the idea of extended families is a distant reality, 'family loyalty' is becoming a thing of the past. In 1993 UNICEF estimated that up to 40 per cent of children in the UK and America had not seen their father for a year. Added to this there is the fact that mobility has increasingly converted us into a commuter society with more of us having our family, work and leisure activities in different locations.

Ironically, mass communications have not helped. In 1993 I listened to a Radio 4 broadcast on the impact of radio on community life. What was once a means of uniting people has now become the cause of a 'fragmented national psyche' as people receive the same information simultaneously in isolated compartments through their personal set. Even the great unifying soap operas like *EastEnders* or *Coronation Street* lock us into the same story in separate mindsets. It is perfectly possible to sit with a family watching the same programme, only to discover that they may watch together without truly sharing the experience.

Much has been made of 'globalisation'. The media gives the impression that our hi-tech communication channels and super-highways bring us into the same room of common concerns, interests and experiences. It is true up to a point. But the greater truth is that our global awareness gives us a stronger picture of diversity and differences. Mass communication usually brings us together to let us know that we are really not the same.

With the challenge to institutional power has come the relativisation of values. The world still carries vivid memories of events surrounding the death of Diana, Princess of Wales. For me, some of the most poignant memories included the sight of the Union Jack at half mast, gently swaying in the summer breeze over Buckingham Palace, and the royal family waiting outside the palace to accompany the princess's cortege. It was the triumph of the people over protocol. The old values were under pressure. In British terms it was a revolution of sorts.

A critical question of our time is: 'Who has the right to say what's right?' As someone once said: 'In our society today the only wrong thing is to claim you are right!' In this twilight zone of ethical and moral relativism we may be almost certain that there are absolutely no absolutes. This affects everything around us. It tampers with our understanding of truth and gives us a greater range of spiritual realities to choose from. It is the pick-and-mix culture in which our right to choose has ensured that the sovereignty of personal choice has become an equal contender with our corporate responsibilities.

Ravi Zacharias, the international apologist, tells the story of his visit to Ohio University. He was shown around the world's first post-modern building based on a non-functional design where window frames and doors were placed unconventionally and stairs led to nowhere in particular. His question to the students was very simple: 'Did they do the same thing to the foundations?' It seems they did not. The problem with so much of our contemporary culture is that the foundations appear to be breaking up.

This brief social sketch is not a doom-and-gloom story of evangelical piety. There are still millions of good and caring people in Britain who will give to good causes, feed their neighbour's cat and become distressed if their favourite

TV character is on the wrong end of a scripted injustice. Big themes about justice and the environment fuel our energies and move us to action. But in this troubled sea, the Church seeks to navigate a stable course. And in these uncertain waters modern Christianity will inevitably encounter many choppy swirls in the years ahead.

It is true that 'no man is an island'; it is just that some larger islands may find that fact difficult to believe, and organisational continents sometimes need a lot of convincing. In my early stages as the General Secretary of the African and Caribbean Evangelical Alliance, it became very clear that one of the problems in getting groups together was invariably the fact that they had become large and fairly self-sufficient. Often I heard fellow ministers bemoaning the fact that they had not seen so-and-so for a long time, when they used to meet more often 'in the early days'. Life had simply become busy with the relative success of growth. People with whom they once had close working relationships were rapidly becoming distant. To some extent this was a story of success, but many church leaders had not learned to handle this kind of development and did not make space to keep in touch with others beyond the gravitational pull of their own very busy church agendas. This was, in part, the nature of the work I felt called to: the quiet cementing of relationships around shared convictions and objectives, providing forums and frameworks in which key leaders could think and work together beyond their own boundaries.

Any attempt to work within the rich diversity of the evangelical Church would need to take seriously the cost of relative success. Evangelicalism is no longer a besieged and nervous part of the Christian community. Still marginalised within the wider British society, it has, however, enjoyed a measure of profile and success which has led to a new-found confidence. And while there has been decline in church attendance over the last two decades, the evangelical Church has shown signs of development both in attendance and in community-based activities. The Alliance's survey of its own churches in the run-up to the Assembly in 1996 showed that 53 per cent of local churches had grown over a twelve-month period. Networks within this growth area of Christian commitment have inevitably shown an enterprising flair for new ideas, greater vision and novelty in community care, social action, evangelism and prayer. Indeed, one of the features of denominations and networks has been the tendency to take on activities in these areas of work which were once the sole province of para-church groups. Recent history has shown that the best models now include those ideas and ministries which serve the individual drive of the local church. In this respect March for Jesus and Alpha have been good examples of this trend.

It soon became evident to me that an important starting point in keeping the disparate parts of our community together was to continue to serve and affirm its diversity, encouraging successful models while still pointing them to the bigger picture. Also we had to keep our eyes on some of the very real tensions which were likely to keep us apart. Most of these tensions were clustered around evangelical commitment to the Bible and its meaning for us in the modern world. The central struggle has invariably been the problem of separating our own cultural position from the genuine concern for biblical truth. This has been at the centre of a growing hermeneutical debate among all Christians who want to take the Word and the world seriously.

The difficulty is that none of us can step outside our culture to become instantly objective in our view of the world. In the same way that I saw non-Pentecostals through my own spiritual and cultural lenses, we must all see through the cultural windows of our spiritual domestication. It is an issue which has attracted a great deal of attention for those involved in missions, but increasingly for all of us who want to be true to the Bible and relevant to those around us. Evangelical diversity will continue to struggle with this for years to come.

It became evident to me that the issue I had been struggling with for many years was in fact the substance of much evangelical and Christian controversy: how do we decipher biblical truth from our own cultural positions on a range of issues? There was an old cultural dominance driven by a systematic, rational approach which had come to determine reliable biblical truth. Generalisations are always difficult, but there is a tendency for conservative/ Reformed evangelicals, schooled in a level of intellectual rigour, to be prescriptive and intolerant of other evangelical viewpoints. Thus, an intellectually coherent and predictable position can be confused with 'truth'. Sadly, this attitude leads to an impenetrable mindset which responds without listening to others and which can become intolerant in the name of truth. The greater sadness is that other parts of the evangelical Church often need these keen theological insights which have been detached from genuine encounter, except for polemic purposes. The problem is that this approach to Christianity is increasingly being regarded as the province of privileged middle-class scholars and church leaders from established traditions.

It didn't take me very long to work out why evangelicals from the Celtic nations warmly endorsed my appointment as UK Director and later as General Director. I hope they felt I had the relevant ministry attributes, but it was also clear that they were affirming the vote for cultural diversity along with many other parts of the evangelical world. Culture is important. We saw this as we worked together to arrange our EA celebrations across the UK to celebrate the

150th anniversary of the EA. Again and again it became an important theme in speaking to Asian Christians or with members of the Black church community. But it was equally significant to younger Christians who came from a different and radical sub-culture, who found the Church extremely tiresome and difficult to understand.

Within the community of evangelical Christian faith the tensions between a more cerebral and 'conservative' culture as opposed to a more intellectually open and celebratory culture showed up in a variety of ways. Invariably these had much to do with different levels of tolerance around issues to do with biblical truth. Nowhere was this more clearly seen than in the difficult and protracted discussions about Morris Cerullo.

Morris Cerullo, the American evangelist, had visited the UK annually for over thirty years before launching his high-profile Mission to London in 1990. From the late 1960s his ministry attracted significant numbers of people across the capital to what had become the largest and most consistent annual evangelistic gathering in the UK for many years; his annual meetings filled the Westminster Central Hall before moving to the Royal Albert Hall. His formal launch of Mission to London drew some 15,000 people to Earls Court. It was accompanied by a high-profile advertising campaign which drew attention to his particular style and cultural approach, but also to the fact that MTL was a member of the Evangelical Alliance. It kept us all very busy.

His gatherings were led by a variety of international Pentecostals, some of whom were from the UK. There was a heavy emphasis on healing, a strong evangelistic appeal linked with a vibrant culture of celebration. Historically, his meetings had been supported mainly by African and Caribbean Pentecostals. Cerullo was not everyone's cup of coffee. He was from the classical Pentecostal mould, but not all Pentecostals were particularly happy with his approach. By far the most universally disliked feature of his ministry was his approach to fund-raising which caused a great deal of dissent even from sections of the community who supported his ministry. Appeal letters appeared in rapid succession, and for many individuals they came very close to a kind of modern-day 'indulgence', offering healing or financial prosperity as a direct result of supporting his work.

The controversy aroused by this high-profile member of the EA was very demanding. Personally I also found it very difficult. As a Pentecostal, Cerullo had been a very important feature in my formative Christian development. In my early teens, he had challenged me to take God seriously and had done much to sustain my faith in a God of miracles against the tidal wave of secular cynicism which so readily dismissed the miraculous. I too had made the annual visit to Central Hall and experienced the heightened sense of expectation that God would actually do something among people who expected Him to work. I saw miracu-lous episodes of healing and heard highly inspirational sermons which elevated faith in God. Even in those days, though, it was very evident that Morris had a slight impatience with the average church and Bible 'seminary'.

We knew that the EA membership of Mission to London would be difficult. What it highlighted was the extent to which cultural clash and biblical concerns came together in the debate. Morris's Americanisms got in the way of serious debate. In the initial stages we had to work very hard to get beyond the objections to his American tele-evangelist dramatics. The debate, which lasted until his resignation in 1996, also exposed the extent to which British Christianity was nervous about the idea of a God of miracles. For many years, nothing in British evangelicalism had so fired debate, in public or private, about a God of miracles. The fact that African and Caribbean Christians were the main support-base for Morris's ministry was in itself an important feature. These were not necessarily the unthinking end of the evangelical spectrum. They included many professionals and university students. It did suggest, though, that these Christians found the emphasis on miracles far less difficult than did other sections of our membership. Rightly or wrongly, they were less concerned about the politics of the events and belonged to a theological and experiential culture in which the idea of God's immediate intervention in the concept of worship was more readily accepted.

For these people, earnest and dedicated in their service of God, Morris's ministry was an acceptable model which infringed neither their understanding of biblical imperatives nor their own cultural grid. He too believed in the inspiration of the Bible – believed it fundamentally and, more than most, spoke uncompromisingly against liberal Christianity. Morris did not deny the Virgin birth, the deity of Christ or the Trinity. He accepted the ministry and vicarious work of Christ, His true death and resurrection. He spoke with confidence about the ascension and stood firmly in the classical Pentecostal position on the Second Coming of Christ. People were helped and healed in the meetings; thousands went home encouraged to see God as a financial provider, filled with faith to face another day. When we spoke about problems with his evangelical credentials they found it very hard to understand. They could not see what all the fuss was about. They were less inclined to ask questions about cultural sensitivities, or frequent and forceful appeals based on the tentative handling of Bible texts. When they looked at the story of Elijah and the widow of Zarephath (1 Kgs. 17:13–16) they could not understand why Morris could not say something similar. Our discussions about accountability and credibility became lost in the cultural cross-fire.

The Cerullo story serves as a good example of those

things which will inevitably press us in years to come as we find a legitimate course between cultural colouring and biblical truth. Unless significant and growing sections of the Christian community are to be excluded from a legitimate place within biblical Christianity in Britain, these will be issues which stay with us indefinitely. Most growing churches in Britain, who gather around the fundamental points of the historic Christian creeds, now include Christians drawn from African and Asian communities. Like the Cerullo story, their challenge to British evangelicalism will not be the removal of its old landmarks but some additions.

Whereas British Christianity has been nervous to admit any relationship between faith and finance, many of these growing churches will bring a proper challenge for us to consider a more balanced response to biblical giving and tithing. My experience is that many Christian churches, fearful of appearing greedy and extortionate, go out of their way to play it down, emphasising that the offering is 'only for the members'. In many Black churches the offering is an open invitation to 'give sacrificially' with a reminder that 'God will pour out a blessing on you'. Similarly, many churches preach the Gospel with a quiet, impersonal invitation to respond – if one is given at all. Most African–Caribbean groups, and growing numbers of others, offer a very bold invitation to respond to the preached word. 'God can heal you now!' is an addition to the altar appeal which is neither wrong nor right, but which would never be heard in some churches and is frequently heard in others. These developments will need to be tested biblically, but they may also need to be sifted culturally. The spiritual skill will be to ensure that we do not confuse the two.

Over the past three years I have had reason to reflect much more on the supposed dichotomy between the idea of unity and truth. The Alliance's claim to represent unity and truth among evangelicals is indeed a very tall order and it is not surprising that it has attracted a certain amount of suspicion from some quarters. The concern has been that people like me, who have a passion for unity on the widest possible evangelical platform, must inevitably obtain unity at the expense of truth. The concern is rightly for the preservation of biblical truth rather than the acquisition of numbers for their own sake.

Indeed if my Sunday morning interviewer was not to be proven right, this was bound to be a very important issue for British evangelicals. Throughout my first year in the new appointment two responses to this issue became very meaningful to me. The first was from my colleague and General Secretary in Northern Ireland, David McCarthy, for whom unity, particularly in the complexities of the Northern Irish context, had become such a cardinal issue. In his own thoughts, any attempt to limit unity merely to gathering around a group of biblical ideas was in effect to diminish the power of biblical unity. David was quite convinced that the truth, which was to be the focal point of our unity, was the person of Jesus Himself. True unity was therefore inextricably bound up with a true relationship with Jesus, who is truth. The same was true for Arfon Jones, then General Secretary of the Alliance in Wales. Arfon, for whom the Welsh language and identity has been a consuming passion over many years, was equally convinced that our unity in Christ is an essential starting point for evangelical unity.

Personally I was attracted to this cry for unity which was the hallmark of ACEA's ministry. Experience would suggest that a commitment to biblical unity is likely to help us in our understanding of the truth. It is surely the drawing together of the experiences, insights and perspectives of those who have been touched by the resurrected Christ, drawn by His Spirit and brought before

His Word which gives us any claim to biblical unity.

Biblical unity begins with an inclusiveness around the genuine work of the cross. This is properly understood in the historic community of believers who have come to recognise those things which are fundamental to our relationship with the risen Christ and those things He may still wish to teach us by His Spirit through each other. It will be a tension which we experience time and again, for the relationship between truth and unity will never be a comfortable one. Almost inevitably, some section of the Church will take it upon themselves to declare what truth looks and sounds like in all circumstances and for all time.

It was this very conviction which brought together the Alliance's Commission on Unity and Truth among Evangelicals to study together the difficult and growing debate about prosperity and the Gospel. In this forum, Hugh Osgood, Senior Pastor of Cornerstone Christian Forum, made a presentation on 'Prosperity Teaching and Evangelical Unity' which suggested that we look closely both at truth and at our ability to stand together *by* the truth of our experience with Christ, *for* the truth of our essential biblical convictions; that we consider the truth *on which we stand* in separating essentials from personal preferences, and the truth *in which we stand* which continues to grow with our relationships and study.

To put it another way, true Christian faith is held by the truth of what God has done in us through faith in Christ. All Christians who encounter this truth grow to recognise the historic claims of the Christian doctrines which we defend. It is on this assurance of faith that we stand to bear witness to the truth by words and practice. But we also recognise that this truth in which we stand together changes and deepens as we learn from each other and are instructed by experience and personal maturity. When I left LBC I had discovered that many evangelicals were not like me but were, nonetheless, held by the same truth of life in Christ. And although we differed in many ways, we stood for the same essential truths about Jesus, His nature, death and resurrection. I have also discovered over the years that washing or not washing the saints' feet is in a very different order of priorities in the scheme of biblical truth.

Our future unity in Christ will be protected by our steadfast agreement on those essentials where the Bible leaves us in no doubt, but we will continue to provide a rod for our backs if we draw a narrow circle on the basis of our own cultural preferences and call it the ring of truth. Biblical unity cannot be entirely prescriptive, because truth is more than sterile doctrinal assent to credal statements. It has as much to do with revealed doctrinal truth (John 17:17–21) as it does with the glory of God (John 17:22). It goes without saying that God's truth cannot be separated from His glory but it is also hard to disguise the fact that they are not quite the same thing. In fact the whole thrust of John 17, and his Gospel in general, is the relational aspect of truth. No one can read John chapters 14 to 17 without recognising that the unity of which the Bible speaks is more than a set of propositions. It is profoundly relational, and relational in such a way that it does not abandon doctrine. It is not either or; it is both and.

It appears that we are at a very important intersection as we approach the new millennium: the point between a growing popular distrust of the old science of rationality and the new triumph of existentialism. In other words, people now pay attention to and value their feelings more than ever before. The new message has been encapsulated by the advertising slogans which scream at us on a daily basis. As the Nike advert suggested, 'Just do it!' I was really taken back by the blatant message which came through a Sprite advert last year. It ran something like this:

What do really gorgeous people drink when they are
really thirsty?
The same as everyone else.
Image is nothing.
Thirst is everything.
Obey your thirst!

When I learned Christian apologetics I was taught classical
arguments for the existence of God. These were reasoned
explanations, using the tools of rational thinking to demonstrate that it was feasible to believe in God. They were not
really proofs of God's existence, but they appealed to
common sense, arguing that our intuitive moral behaviour,
the order of the universe and design in nature all point to
God's existence. In our effort to establish the credibility of
Scripture, evangelicals learned to meet the 'scientific'
challenge of biblical criticism with reasoned evidence drawn
from archaeology and clear thinking to counteract scholarship which appeared to undermine the Bible. But today,
the ground is shifting. People are beginning to trust their
intuitive feelings as much as their minds. Truth may be on
the big screen or simply 'out there'. Even in the corporate
world, the old harsh models of masculine productivity and
cold performance indexes are giving way to a softer, pastoral
approach in which the feelings and well-being of the work-
force have become important. Evangelicalism, brought up
on classical arguments of reasoned defence, will always have
its place in Christian witness. The challenge before us is
not to abandon reason but to develop a flexibility which
makes us as comfortable about our experience of God as
our arguments about God. And there is no doubt about it;
experience is in.

I still remember the extent to which my social work
training encouraged me to find out how people felt. 'What
are you feeling about this?' was a standard question. Refusal

to engage with your feelings would be tantamount to a form of 'denial'. With the upsurge in charismatic worship which – with some notable exceptions – has elevated choruses above the more contemplative culture of hymn-singing, it would appear that serious Christian thought is being replaced by a mushy, 'happy-clappy' experientialism. The danger we face together at this point is in assuming that there is any inherent conflict between our minds and our emotions as avenues by which God comes to meet with us. The Bible has numerous examples to show this, such as the story of the eunuch who came to faith as he had the Bible explained to him (Acts 8:26-38). It is equally important to remember that Paul's initial meeting with Jesus came through a dramatic and personal encounter (Acts 9:1–9). We will continue to need a Gospel which is embarrassed about neither the Bible nor our personal experiences of God.

The demands of our contemporary culture have pushed us to the point where successful witness must learn to become culturally bilingual. I learned to glide naturally between two cultures as a youngster – as do thousands of young people today in our multicultural society. In the same way, the Church must develop an ability to speak to the culture of its day without losing its identity. We must work with equal fluidity between the questions of the rational mind and our society's raw emotions. We must have the ability Paul displayed in talking with the rational Stoics and experiential Epicureans of his day (Acts 17). As Ravi Zacharias put it: 'We can find points of reference philosophically, but we must also find points of reference existentially.' Our ability to avoid the fracture between a kind of right brain/left brain approach to Christian faith is destined to be a very important challenge as we face the white waters of fragmentation which already swirl around us in the evangelical Church. What is more, we will have to find a way of doing this which avoids the temptations of intellectual superiority from a cerebral Christian community, or indeed the smug unteachable spirit which so often comes from the conviction that we have 'sussed out' society and now have a few things to say to the sleeping, historic Church.

So in my travels I have been conscious of this very real tension between the two approaches to Christian witness in the modern world. We are walking a tightrope between intellectual indifference to our culture and an over-identification with that culture.

In the first instance, the indifference is caused by sheer inertia or the sense that things are happening at such a rapid pace that we cannot hope to keep abreast of developments in our fast-moving world. With such a mindset it is far easier to opt out; to go for a nostalgic approach to the Church and the world which bemoans the passing of our Judaeo-Christian culture and which longs to turn the clock back. It is true too that many people who sit in this camp – especially church leaders – do so out of a genuine loyalty to old values; they fear that movement in any direction will result in a theological compromise. It is the fear of the long slide down into apostasy.

A growing army of more contemporary Christians, comfortable with technology and in tune with modern culture, have grown impatient with the status quo. They are making their way across the landscape, meandering between the new language and values with such consummate ease that their distinctive features may not always be easily identified at first glance. They are comfortable in cinemas and theatres, they may even smoke and use words their parents would not approve of. They do believe the Bible, but they may not believe it like most people who call themselves evangelicals. In fact, they may prefer to be called 'post-evangelical', if they use the label at all.

Both are caricatures of extreme positions, neither of which commend themselves as helpful models of confident proclamation in the twenty-first century. Somewhere between those two possibilities lies the creative tension of an effective evangelicalism which is unashamed of both the Gospel it preaches and the history of which it is an integral part, but which understands the issues of the day; a clear witness which speaks with clarity and conviction from its privileged relationship with a living Christ, yet which is prepared to enter the joys and desperations of its friends and neighbours. Anything less is a denial of the Gospel and ceases to be truth.

Of course all of this kind of speculation works very well in theory. It is one thing to talk about speaking with clarity and confidence; the difficulty is deciding which things hold us together as primary issues – those points of faith around which we simply cannot afford to differ – as opposed to the things about which we may freely argue.

This very significant issue lies at the heart of what it means to be an evangelical Christian in today's world. It is an issue to which we will return in the next chapter. The point here is that all things in faith and practice cannot carry equal weight if we are to make any sense of our legitimate diversity. The task is to do the tough work about agreeing on those irreducible minimums of authentic Christian faith.

I have to admit that much of my time at the EA has been spent in heated debates about minutiae, about points of distinction and some intractable theological conflicts. But I have seldom heard of any hard work being done to reaffirm the great themes which unite us in faith and about which we would never agree to differ. Such an exercise would be more than the ratifying of our own internalised preferences or our denominational basis of faith.

I have in mind a far more dynamic undertaking in which

evangelicals would sit together across our diverse streams to underscore and renew an affirmation of the things which have clearly become indispensable to our faith. I will also be the first to admit that such an aspiration is likely to be over-simplistic and that two thousand years of church history tell us, if nothing else, that such things are not simply done. But it seems to me that it is too important not to attempt. A steadfast single-mindedness about primary biblical values would indeed be an incredible undertaking but I suspect it would do a great deal to concentrate the evangelical mind and have a liberating impact on our diversity.

Because we are in such a profoundly spiritual environment it has become, and will continue to be, a very important issue for evangelical Christians in contemporary Britain. The UK may have become post-Christian without necessarily becoming post-spiritual. The obvious new influx has been the growth of charismatic and Pentecostal spirituality which has made such a deep impression on all sections of church life across the traditions. Through the charismatic renewal and the worship culture which became its main conduit, this kind of spirituality has been evident from the more reserved evangelical churches to Catholic services.

There has also been an increasing move towards a more contemplative style of spirituality with a renewed interest in Taizé worship and the Iona Community pointing to a lower decibel culture. At the General Synod in July 1998 members were somewhat taken back by what Tony Higton had to say. Rev. Higton, formerly a champion of the anti-homosexual lobby in Synod, announced that he would no longer make this a focus of his work. What really came as a surprise to members of the Synod was his appeal to the Church to open its mind to the helpful symbols beyond Christianity which could play a part in our spirituality. He noted, for example, that while he did not believe in the healing properties of crystals, he regarded them as useful aids to meditation and inner-healing. There was no suggestion that Tony was moving away from orthodox Christianity but it was surprising that a leading Anglican evangelical, who had himself written about the dangers of the New Age, was willing to pay attention to the helpful opportunities which their symbolisms might have for Christian worship.

It is unlikely that we will have lost this tendency to learn from and borrow from the symbolisms and icons of our contemporary society. In an effort to reach it and bring meaning to its emptiness we are increasingly likely to run the risk of embracing new forms of spirituality which we would not have contemplated earlier. The new interest in forms of Celtic worship and Christianity which have emerged in recent years has certainly been an indication of a genuine desire to build helpful footpaths to allow the community to beat a path to the Christian Church. There are those who remain concerned that the Church should not get lost among its own paving stones.

Between January and March 1998 we conducted a tour in twenty-six centres across the UK. Seizing the Moment was very hard work but it was also very satisfying, providing as it did the opportunity to meet with nearly 2,000 church leaders in the Alliance's membership. The tour was a direct outflow of our time together in the 1996 Assembly in which we promised that we would pursue the commitment we made to develop the main points in our Declaration.

An integral part of our tour was to hear from church leaders who came to be with us at each venue: we asked the same questions twenty-six times. One of our important questions was to find out what they saw as the obstacles to our unity. The unanimous consensus at the top of our list was tensions between charismatics and non-charismatic Christians.

The feedback was an affirmation of my own experience. There were a variety of mildly anti-charismatic complaints which had come to us over the years – some of which have some justifications. Frankly, charismatics were often up against it from Pentecostal as well as conservative leaders. Sometimes charismatic leaders were challenged by other charismatic leaders: charismatics were at the centre of the Toronto phenomenon; they had brought in an unhelpful Wimber weakening of the baptism of the Holy Spirit; they had too often enjoyed the limelight even though they were still relatively small numerically; they had weakened the theology of hell, replacing it with an annihilationist position, and they had supported the ultra-Armenianism of Clark Pinnock's 'Openness theology', suggesting that God changes His behaviour and His mind as a direct result of our petition. Charismatics were guilty of repeated prophetic claims which had gone unchecked and unchallenged and often led others astray. In fact, one senior conservative evangelical leader once said he was very happy with Pentecostals as opposed to charismatics. 'I don't agree with everything they say,' he said, 'but at least I know what they are about. It's these charismatics I can't work out.'

The popular perception was that the Alliance was overtaken by charismatic Christianity and was therefore in danger of being swept away by a charismatic activist culture which would ultimately weaken the integrity of the Gospel we all claimed to obey.

The reality is that charismatic experience has been the dominant factor in recent years. In spite of its flaws it has been a strong influence behind significant movements such as Spring Harvest and March for Jesus. It has also been a driving force in international movements for world evangelism such as DAWN and has dominated international prayer movements. Its culture has been so persuasive that where it has met with its older spiritual cousins, the Pentecostal movement, it has made a marked impression upon it and infiltrated both Black and White expressions of Pentecostalism. It is easy to enter some Pentecostal churches without knowing whether they are Pentecostal or charismatic. It is estimated that between 75 amd 80 per cent of those who have come to faith in Christ around the world in the last three decades have done so through a Pentecostal/charismatic church group and that over 47 per cent of Christians in the UK would now claim to have some kind of charismatic experience. It has surmounted denominational boundaries and spilled out from the confines of its own earlier prejudices against sections of the Christian community. Gerald Coates, leader of the Pioneer group of New Churches, would presumably have been shocked if anyone had predicted twenty years ago that one of his own songs would have been included in a formal Kenyan liturgy for the 1998 SOMA (Sharing Of Ministries Abroad) Conference in Canterbury, just ten days before one of the most significant Lambeth Conferences of the twentieth century!

But the charismatic movement has not been perfect and there are signals that its leaders are experiencing all the challenges of institutionalised Christianity as they too settle in for the long haul. The new openness has also brought its own challenge for quality control, as more and more home songs are spun out and offered to a wider audience. It is true too that the proliferation of prophetic utterances will continue to need a watchful eye as people continue to speak on God's behalf with scant attention to any criteria for authentic reliability. As a church leader who spends much time in so many different settings and absorbs so many prophetic statements, I see a more disturbing factor. It is that so little of this increased volume of prophecy is making any apparent difference to the real world beyond our churches. Even for those of us who are not charismatic, it is hard to deny the influence of the charismatic movement on modern Christianity. But if prophecy has been a gift, it is one we must all take better care of.

I stood entranced by what was happening during my very first visit to New Frontiers International conference in 1994. NFI was in the midst of the Toronto phenomenon. What was encouraging to see was the steady and clear exposition of Scripture presented by Terry Virgo in response to the events which had overtaken the movement. But not even the clear Bible teaching could hold back the weight of this unusual set of events. Before he finished his teaching there was a gentle and irrepressible outbreak of laughter splashing like a gently rising wave across the giant shed in Stoneleigh. I saw amazingly bizarre sights those two days I was with them. In some cases, the body language said all that needed to be said. In other instances, I was helped only by the subsequent testimony of the person concerned or from someone else who helped me understand the significance of what had taken place. At the end of one session someone offered to pray with me. It was not the first time I had ever fallen to the floor: that's where I had ended up when I experienced my surcharge of divine love as a nineteen-year-old Christian in my home church. I was fully conscious, treated with very careful dignity and allowed to lie quietly listening to the array of voices around me. No great transitions took place. I was simply resting at a depth I had not known for a while.

My last visit to Stoneleigh in 1996 was quieter. But there was a new interest in a development taking place in America. There was talk of thousands of people coming to repentance and personal faith in Christ in a hitherto unknown Assemblies of God church in Pensacola. Apparently, this was revival.

Closer to home, Christians in Wales, who for the past three hundred years have seen a revival in every generation except this one, are eager for another revival. Stoneleigh and the Evangelical Movement in Wales are not the only ones hungry for revival. Most Christians are. Evangelicalism is unintelligible without the concept of revival. Both movements, though very different in their approach and with very different horizons, are Calvinist but would differ in their experience and expectations of what revival would look like. Both are hungry for God to move in unprecedented ways.

But there is also a debate as to how God may bring revival and whether in fact we are in revival. There is no doubting the fact that God is doing great things among us. There are great stories to tell of full and successful churches, expanding buildings and visionary projects. The growth of Alpha courses and the great movements in prisons are both very good news for the Gospel. But there is another story. Behind the notable pockets of optimism we are losing significant ground as church attendance continues to decline and the Christian values have less influence on policy-makers in a multi-value society. Most of us would agree that we are in urgent need of God's help.

AMEN! A Day to Pray was a UK-wide prayer initiative which drew together a wide range of churches in a day of prayer in June 1998. Revival was one of four themes on which we focused our prayers. The problem was that for a number of individuals there could be no revival without repentance. It seemed odd to me that we could have such a mechanistic view of how God works, particularly when history has examples of God moving without invitation to renew and restore His Church. It would be a pity to lock ourselves into an unnecessary tension between repentance and/or revival. So often it is the awakening of the human spirit through revival which leads us into repentance, while at other times it is only our obedient humility that will move God's heart on our behalf. At the end of the day it is in seeking God through prayer that we are either revived or led to true acts of repentance.

The world in which we live will throw up many challenges to our witness as a Bible community. The question is not whether we will be allowed an audience in a society with so many voices on offer. The real question is whether we will prevent ourselves from being heard by the interminable noise of our 'important' internal arguments. If British evangelicalism is to enter a new millennium stronger than ever we must all remain conscious of the hidden doubts behind my interviewer's question. With such a wide range of opinions and issues, can we really stay together?

8

A Question of Identity

In October 1996 I joined over two hundred church leaders at the Boddington Hotel in London at a conference hosting Myles Munroe. Myles, noted internationally as a very powerful motivational speaker and writer, was addressing the theme 'Twenty-first Century Leadership: Impacting the Nation'. The meeting was notable for its mixture of Black and White church leaders who had gathered to hear Myles. The heart of his address was essentially an appeal to unity in diversity but in this particular talk he was asked to deal specifically with leadership. His starting point was a little surprising. 'The greatest issue of the twenty-first century,' he suggested, 'is the question of identity. The first question of the human heart is: Who am I?'

He was right. I first became conscious of the importance of self-knowledge as a sixth-former during weekend work filling shelves in Tesco. I wandered into the store room one day to be confronted with a small plaque which said: 'The knowledge of yourself will preserve you from vanity.' For some reason it had always felt as though that notice had been placed in that spot as a personal note to me!

But it was certainly the question which had come home to me with intense weight during my time at London Bible College all those years earlier. The question did not go away when I left college. It was still there before me during two years of social work training between 1977 and 1979 and into my period of service as a probation officer. I had never come across the notion of 'identity crisis' before my training. It was the term used to describe the social trauma of adolescence in the years between puberty and adulthood, or the social tensions of people who had to work through layers of sub-culture in their process of coming to terms with exactly who or what they were. I saw it exhibited on a regular basis in my clients' experiences. In some cases it was an issue facing children born to mixed parents who had to work out whether they were 'Black' or 'White'. In some instances, young African men in the criminal justice system found it easier to pose as cultural Caribbeans to fall in with popular stereotypes. In fact, some of them became more Caribbean than Caribbeans! Identity was also an issue for Black children brought up in foster homes or institutions.

But it wasn't all about ethnicity. Mostly it had to do with belonging. I recall a young woman on probation who came to see me for an initial meeting looking and sounding very 'well to do'. My seventeen-year-old secretary was not impressed and marked her off as an ordinary working-class girl 'all tarted up' to impress. It appeared that her handbag was a give-away. Her subsequent visits vindicated my secretary's perceptiveness. Her handbag was indeed a little worn around the edges. It betrayed her, and her posh accent caved in under pressure. It was what the textbooks had described as an identity crisis. She wanted to be what she was not.

Having studied the issue of self-awareness I began to recognise that, along with many others from an ethnic background, this was an integral part of my own journey as a Black Britisher in more ways than one. Having married in 1976, Carol and I had our two children. Our son, Joel Junior, was born in 1978 and our daughter, Davina, in 1982.

For both of them, their transition to self-awareness was identical. Neither had problems with self-perception before going to school. Evidently, they thought of themselves at home and in church simply as children. School brought a new level of awareness. Questions about their colour, home life and weekend activities showed that they were different. The extent of this self-discovery became particularly pronounced when our daughter gave her evaluation of our colour after primary school one evening. 'Me, Joel and Mum are all brown,' she said. And then pointing directly at me she said: 'You are Black.' It gave us something to talk about that evening but also demonstrated the level of self-awareness which thousands of British children from a range of backgrounds have gone through in the development of a multicultural Britain.

In my case, self-awareness wasn't just about colour and culture. My work in the broader Christian Church was not readily understood or even approved of. Few said it, but it was evident that the direction in which my ministry had gone did not meet with total comprehension or approval. Few people within the world of Black Pentecostalism really understood the complexity or diverse nature of evangelical Christianity. My work as General Secretary of the African and Caribbean Evangelical Alliance was in part to create better understanding and mutual awareness between that important part of the Christian community and the wider Church in Britain. There were those who became totally convinced that I had abandoned my past, had lost my true identity, and was setting off in the wrong direction. I worked on the assumption that it was perfectly possible to maintain my identity, remain positive about my cultural heritage and yet be culturally bilingual. The ability to speak a different cultural language had become a natural part of my own spiritual, intellectual and cultural upbringing. I discovered that I did not subscribe to the school of thought which

A Question of Identity

venerated a romanticised Blackness. I had worked out that
I was happy not to be English. I was coming to rest with
the reality that I was a Black Britisher who knew more
about London than he did about Jamaica. But I also knew
that I was not the same kind of Jamaican as my mother and
that I shared a Britishness which my spiritual parents did
not. It was part pain and part pleasure. And I had grown to
know a bigger, broader God. A God who called me to
work in a wider field than I had hitherto realised existed. It
was not always comfortable but it was right.

Myles' point about identity was not the main point of
his presentation but it certainly stuck with me. Events in
world affairs have underscored his point. Since the Second
World War nearly all wars across the world have continued
to be internal battles over identity and belonging. It has
become a major preoccupation of the columnists in the
British press, and the flames of national pride and self-
determination have been fuelled by everything from the
unhelpful naivety of the former chair of the Conservative
party, Lord Tebbit (who matched nationality with who
spectators cheer for at an international cricket match) to
the complex debates on devolution. With the advent of
two significant votes for elements of political autonomy in
Scotland and Wales, and with the significant political initiatives in Northern Ireland, the real debate has had much to
do with the elusive quest for the identity of 'Englishness'.
Headlines such as 'Englishness slips away' (*Guardian*, 16 Sept.
1997), 'Proud to be British'(*New Statesman*, 26 June 1998)
and 'Farewell to England's nation state' (*Daily Telegraph*, 29
June 1998) tell the story of Britain's new search for cultural,
political and social cohesion. Perhaps nothing demonstrated
this quite as much as the 1998 World Cup. It was fascinating
to see widespread appreciation of the Jamaican Reggae
Boyz across the UK, but it was equally telling to see the
extent to which the other nations of the United Kingdom

set themselves apart from the English – particularly in the fans' behaviour. As one columnist suggested, the main reason Scottish fans were so well behaved during the World Cup series was to avoid being identified with the English!

In our multi-layered, multi-choice Britain it is hardly surprising that the Christian Church is also asking profound questions about its own identity. Drawn from an ever-expanding range of experiences, denominations and groups, contemporary Christianity in general and evangelical faith in particular must inevitably struggle with the question of its own identity.

Questions about identity are inevitable. In any pilgrimage new landmarks and encounters will force us to ask important questions of ourselves. The very fact that we are thrown up against the political, social and spiritual realities of a world must involve us in the process of change and definition. Not everyone welcomes the evangelical meltdown which is upon us in Britain. Lines and boundaries are not as clearly drawn as they once were. We meet each other more often through the ever-expanding conference circuits and growing number of publications. They bring us into close proximity but also sharpen the contrasts, showing up the things which make us different even when we still hold to the same fundamentals. Short of a new monasticism, I was unable to avoid the encounters which came my way, shaping and correcting my own unhelpful attitudes to those I hardly understood and with whom I could happily disagree at a distance. As I found at London Bible College, close encounters often change people although they do not always change their basic beliefs.

It is as we mirror each other around the Bible and in the context of worship that the questions of our identity will be raised again and again. To ask 'What is an evangelical?' is neither a sin nor a weakness of evangelical faith. To treat it as such is to impose unnecessary burdens on ourselves. To suggest, either in words or attitude, that no one else should ask it of us could be arrogant. But it is also important to remember that the question is not new. Since the mid 1990s numerous publications have drawn attention to it. In 1996 the Alliance's Theological Commission's first major publication again raised the question 'What is an evangelical?' with some practical guidelines for consideration. But the question is old. It was certainly raised by Lord Shaftesbury who declared, 'I know what constituted an Evangelical in former times . . . I have no clear notion what constitutes one now.'

And it is worth noting that no less a person than Charles Spurgeon had a very similar problem: 'It is a mere cant to cry, "We are evangelical; we are evangelical" and yet decline to say what evangelical means.'

Evangelicals should not be thrown by the fact that it is a difficult debate. 'Evangelical' is not a synonym for Christian. If heaven is reserved for evangelicals alone then God has a real problem on His hands, for many of us will know of others who do not use the label but who may truly be called 'godly' people. What is God to do with them? So until evangelicals reach the point where we are willing to suggest otherwise we must approach the discussion with much humility. We must be prepared to enter the discussion with strong convictions and a willingness to listen and learn. Our views, however clear to ourselves and those close to us, need not mean that the discussion is cut and dried. 'Evangelical' is not an easy label to wear, any more than 'Christian' is, and we do well to remember that we are a part of a very big debate. It is a debate in which the world stands as curious spectators, confused by the finer points of the arguments but very aware of our body language.

The author and dramatist Dennis Potter once remarked that the problem with words is that you never know where they have been.

The label 'evangelical' has often raised more questions than it solves. When it strays from its more appropriate use as a noun and is used as an adjective it leaves evangelicals open to a range of sad caricatures. To the uninformed it can conjure up images of benign do-gooders insulated by unreality, wagging their fingers at the rest of humanity as one does to an unruly child. It may even smack of a fundamentalism best known for disagreeing with everyone in general and agreeing with no one in particular – except themselves. It may even, in the words of a former archbishop, be 'happy-clappy'. Little wonder that a growing number of younger Christians who may be evangelical by persuasion are increasingly disowning the label.

But while contemporary evangelicalism cannot afford to venerate the word there are those who remain committed to its theological position and to its rehabilitation in modern Christian vocabulary. 'Evangelical' comes from the New Testament Greek word for 'Gospel'. It therefore rests in the true Story of Good News. Our modern word was first associated with the early reformer John Wycliffe – known as 'Doctor Evangelicus' – and later with Martin Luther himself. Evangelical definitions relate very closely to its genesis. An evangelicalism which defines a biblical Christian through the window of the Reformation is likely to draw a narrow circle in which few others may stand. It tends to have a more prescriptive definition and becomes guarded against any definitions which stray too far from a Reformation world view. On the other hand, evangelicals who have come from a post-Reformation and particularly Pentecostal or charismatic position will appeal beyond the Reformation to a definition of an evangelical which includes a wider range of Christians.

My own journey as a Christian pilgrim, through a forest of Christian cultures and perspectives about the Bible, has kept reminding me that I am not always right. But then I am not always wrong either. There have been some things which keep repeating themselves among the people I come across from many nations, cultures and church traditions around the world. I have met people who are very different from me but who have the same convictions which mesh with my reading of the Bible and with whom I share the intangible reality of a life in the Spirit.

And it has been a long journey. I have discovered that those who know nothing of the 'baptism of the Spirit', as I experience and understand it, are also one with me in the same Spirit. And beyond our diverse experiences of Christ and the work of that same Spirit are common beliefs which hold us together in spite of our real differences. Even with these differences there are aspects of faith and practice which I hold on to in common with many other Christians from a wide range of Christian groups.

In establishing parameters for credible Christianity mere conditioning will not do. Like many other Christians from many other traditions, it has not been my practice to go to the cinema or the pub. But after a while these do not seem to be things worth fighting for. Even if I decline the invitation, somehow Christianity seems worthy of greater marks of distinction than these. Similarly, I am now fully convinced that I am unlikely ever to turn up to a regular worship event, either on a Sunday or mid-week, wearing shorts. It still goes against my cultural grain, but I am very unlikely to walk out if others do it. More importantly, I remain theologically convinced that the separation of Church and State is the proper relationship and that adult baptism is clearly mandated in the Bible. But these ceased to be primary issues around which I would withdraw my fellowship from fellow pilgrims within the Christian Church. In time, experience, humility and a good deal of soul-searching have led me to believe that there are bigger issues on which credible Christian faith should be based.

I recently overheard someone singing an old chorus:

> Tell me the old, old story
> Of Jesus and His love.

It was a refreshing reminder of an old song which retains a quaint relevance today. The Story of the Bible is very old and very relevant. In our contemporary culture the great temptation is to put compartments around the whole Story by dividing it into bite-size chunks for popular consumption. The danger is that we tend to miss the big theme. And it is worth fighting to keep it in focus. However we end up making it relevant and credible for those around us, all those entrusted with the Story of Good News simply cannot afford to lose sight of the whole.

It begins with the assertion that God created the world and everything in it. That He called the Jewish people to Himself as a model nation, gave them timeless teachings about Himself and their relationships with each other. That in spite of these people's failings and disobedience He finally 'showed up' in the Person of Jesus who was miraculously fully man and fully God. This Jesus was born of a virgin in first-century Palestine, lived sinless and died for sinners; was crucified, buried, raised from real, physical death and finally ascended back to God to await a day in which all evil will be judged.

The Good News Story is not one of abandonment. It is one of forgiveness and hope. It is one of a God who redeems people, brings them into a personal relationship with Himself through the Spirit in order that they too will become a part of the process by which individuals and communities become reconciled to God. It is an old Story which stays fresh because people will always need to be forgiven and to belong.

In our contemporary climate of growing spirituality, it

may now be argued that any attempt to empty the Story of its miraculous elements has become a sad, outdated approach to the Bible. People are no longer afraid to believe the unusual. The age of rationalistic science which became the measurement of reliability has been partially swept away by a new demand for an other-worldliness, and the appetite has been drip-fed from the steady flow of paranormal TV programmes, sci-fi movies and the growing consumer demand for paranormal realities. In February 1998, the *Daily Mail* conducted a survey from which it concluded that as much as three-quarters of the population were comfortable with paranormal phenomena.

Miracles, like justice, belong to the Story and, increasingly, human sensibilities are accepting this. It is true that miracles don't happen every day down our street, but the compulsion to strip them away from the great Story in order to make it acceptable is not something that credible Christian witness can afford to contemplate without reducing God and His Story to the limits of our comfort zones.

In 1998, I participated in a BBC 5 Live radio interview. The late-night chat show took place under the shadow of the Lambeth Conference and I joined a journalist with expertise on religion, a Christian MP and an ex-president of the Secular Humanist Society on the panel. The debate centred around the place of the Church in society, its declining numbers and issues of moral ethics, with a specific slant towards the debate about homosexuality and the age of consent. Our after-show chat underlined the plight of an evangelical position against the backdrop of our current culture. Basically, the journalist felt that the Church had no right to tell people they were wrong because they did not fit into the consensus – particularly when some of these people were as moral as – and more likeable than – most Christians. Tolerance, in this scheme of things, must become the basis of our consensus morality.

Fundamentalism is still alive and well in tolerant Britain. But it is still true to say that very few of us go out of our way to be marked down as intolerantly fundamental. Because tolerance has become one of the modern hallmarks of civility, few of us would consciously follow any line of argument or behaviour which sets us apart as intolerant. The anniversary of the death of Diana, Princess of Wales, was an important illustration of this. When a vicar told a Sunday School class that Diana had probably gone to hell it made the headlines and BBC Radio 4's *World at One* programme carried the story. Despite a clear explanation, free of jargon, the vicar was put down as an absolutist because he insisted that good works without faith in Christ were not enough. Issues like these will always present us with difficulties when talking to children, but the bottom line was that our culture remains uncomfortable about clear biblical absolutes.

It is a great challenge to a confident Christianity which wishes to speak to our culture simultaneously with conviction and compassion. How can we be heard clearly and convincingly, while acting lovingly? As the twentieth century closes in upon us, we will undoubtedly be reminded of the lamentable examples in history where the Church failed to be truly Christian in its attitude and responses to those with whom it disagreed or those who chose to disagree with it. There are still Christians who make it clear through their publications and letters that they are perfectly prepared to be disagreeable in their disagreements. But most of us are not like that. We too have been pinned down by the weight of the liberal culture of tolerance. We prefer to agree to disagree. Indeed, given Christianity's poor track record in public relations, we have a vested interest in being as nice as anyone else. There is little pleasure in being discordant.

The problem is that Christianity in our present time is

likely to be a morally, spiritually discordant movement. To make a difficult situation worse, evangelical faith which insists that it has a particular view on God's relationship and response to human sin is likely to be called discordant. Martin Luther once said that we must know God as an enemy before we can know Him as a friend. Perhaps the challenge will be to talk about sin, judgment and forgiveness without appearing to enjoy it!

Evangelicals are likely to be theologically discordant not only within the wider Church but also in relation to other faiths.

I was struck by just how uncomfortable this could be when I was asked to participate in a series for the BBC World Service in 1997. The programme, called *What Do Christians Believe?* trawled a wide range of Christian views about the main points of the Christian faith. I was asked how people get to heaven.

'Christians believe that we are put right with God because we accept what Jesus did for us through His death and resurrection.' It was a standard line.

'Does that mean, then, that if I am a Muslim, a Sikh or a Jew I will not get to heaven?' It was a standard question. I remembered that it was the World Service.

'God's first response is one of love,' I suggested. 'The Christian Gospel does not begin with exclusion zones around other faiths. God's 'cosmic generosity' means that He begins with an invitation to all people – although Christians believe that there is something very unique and unrepeatable about what Christ has done on our behalf . . .' The interviewer listened patiently.

'But surely it follows that if I am a Sikh or a Muslim or a Jew I am unlikely to believe in Christ and His cross and therefore by implication I am unlikely to get to heaven?' It was logical.

I did not enjoy the question and did not want to appear

insensitive or discordant. And she would not let me off the hook. I had to explain that this was an integral part of the pain of the Christian Good News: that there was an exclusivity about Christ and His cross and that although God did indeed love everyone, Christians had a responsibility to say that there is no other way to God apart from Christ; that our Christian witness was not merely our ability to say this from a distance but to love and serve those who may even be offended by this apparently intolerant claim. I believed what I had said but I did not enjoy it very much. And I was very glad that a good friend was available to pray me through the emotions of that interview.

Twenty-first-century evangelicalism is unlikely to remain safe if it is to be effective. In the cross-currents of faiths and non-faith, we will find ourselves closer to the demands and difficulties of the first-century Christians who often sounded intolerant without trying. How we serve others insisting on their right to worship while remaining true to our witness will not be easily accomplished in our society.

We don't have to wander too far into the wider Christian Church to discover that there is often an underlying impatience with evangelicals. Sometimes it has been well deserved. We so easily confuse theological certainty and assurance with smugness and ready-made answers. Wider ecumenism can find us predictably irritating. It has a lot to do with evangelical attitudes and the liberal pride of some non-evangelicals who still confuse clear convictions with intellectual poverty.

This was partially my experience at the Churches Together in England conference a few months after my appointment. I had visited in 1992; on this second visit I discovered that British ecumenism was experiencing a renewed focus with plans for the millennium, a renewed focus on prayer. There was a sense of anticipation. But there were those who quietly told me that they were surprised that a director of the Evangelical Alliance would agree to participate as a guest at an ecumenical event in broad daylight! In fact, one person told me that he had switched off immediately I was introduced as an evangelical. He told me that he had already decided what I was about to say before I started talking. I was grateful that he took the trouble to switch on again because I was at pains to say that, while evangelicals did not have all the answers and needed to recover a pilgrim vulnerability, we were not to be crossed off for having some things about which we are unlikely to shift our ground.

If evangelicalism is to survive the traumas of our post-modern mindset, it must continue to believe in the value of fixed points of reference. It is not intolerance for its own sake. It amounts to a confidence in the Story of the Bible. It also refuses to give way on what Christian tradition has understood about the Bible as God's thoughts made known.

Credible Christianity also has room for uncertainty. I grow weary of Christians who have nothing left to learn from God. Even God probably finds it tricky to build relationships with people who never ask any questions. There is no colour in a black and white world. Christians and particularly Christian leaders need to know that it is sometimes OK not to know. Christian certainty does not involve being certain about everything. The Bible league of uncertainty is very impressive. It includes people like David, Job, Jeremiah and Solomon, Peter and Paul. Even Jesus had moments of uncertainty – on the cross, of all places. With the right approach, doubt can be worked into a virtue and a Christianity which tries to pretend it away is likely to come across as an over-enthusiastic second-hand sales-person. There are times when a cry like 'My God, my God! Why have you let me down?' is likely to be far more credible than a safe line such as 'I know He is always with me.' In any event, the first tends to draw more attention.

Our doubts may be about the experiences which have come our way in our travels with God and others around us. They may, in fact, have to do with our theological position. This is always a difficult one. I lived for many years as a closet doubter about aspects of my pre-millennial position. A seven-year Tribulation immediately after the Second Coming seemed very tenuous from the book of Daniel and I was always hard pressed to be confident about it. And I never could work out why God should bind Satan for the thousand years of the millennium to unleash him again before the Battle of Armageddon. My daughter pulled me out of the closet when she asked me to explain it as she couldn't work it out either. But I still believe that Christ will definitely return powerfully in splendour; and yet so suddenly that He will catch some people napping. Credible Christianity should be free not to know everything immediately.

Author and popular speaker Steve Gaukroger once said that doubt is like a tunnel; OK to travel through but not really ideal to stay in. There will be things about which we are not yet certain, but that doesn't make ignorance a virtue. We have an obligation to give meaning as far as possible to the words we use. This has to be true for what some Christians mean by being 'evangelical'.

Evangelical Christianity, as I have suggested, has long been embroiled in conversations about its identity. From various quarters we have been encouraged to consider those non-negotiable elements of Christian distinctives which mark off evangelical faith world-wide.

Very able minds have contributed to the debate in recent decades and have given us a whole range of evangelical essentials. The lists are invariably determined by each writer's own position within evangelicalism and express theological imperatives as much as historic patterns which have some clear rooting in the Bible, such as social action. They include: Church or community, missions, and revival. Although these may not ultimately mark the central character of evangelicalism any more than other expressions of Christian faith there is certainly a clear identification with what has come to be regarded as evangelical Christianity.

Martyn Lloyd-Jones' seminal work on *What is an Evangelical?*, transcribed from his 1971 addresses to the International Fellowship of Evangelical Students, surprised me when I read it. It was not so much the fact that he began by insisting that 'evangelical' is a prefix which makes a Christian an evangelical before a Baptist, Presbyterian or Episcopalian. In his thinking, evangelicals had a 'distrust of reason', avoided ecumenism, took the supernatural, preaching and revival seriously, and rejected any distinction between the clergy and laity. A leading Calvinist, he regarded Calvinism as a secondary issue, along with modes of baptism and views about the millennium.

I realise that my contribution here will be no less inconclusive, but I would see the following biblical distinctives as the marks of evangelical Christian witness. I find it helpful to begin with an acceptance of a traditional approach to the doctrine of the Trinity. Ultimately, it remains a mystery. As Augustine, the great North African theologian of the fifth century, explained it: 'When one asks "What Three?" human speech suffers from a great lack of power. Nevertheless, we say: "Three Persons" not in order that we should say this but that we should not be silent.'

And yet it was the first significant theological formula which made sense of the relationship between the expressions of God in the world. It tells us of His commitment to the most fundamental aspect of our personhood – the ability to relate. It was a major battle for thinking Christianity and while it must always stretch us beyond our capacity to understand it, it is indispensable to biblical orthodoxy. It tells us about belonging. Trinitarianism is not the sole province of evangelical faith, but there is no theological harm done in standing with others on this important point of historic orthodoxy.

But because 'evangelical' is a Gospel word evangelicals must take the Bible seriously. So many have helped us see this as foundational to the credible Christianity to which evangelicalism aspires. The commitment to biblical authority has to be one of our non-negotiable points. By 'authority' we must mean that the Bible is regarded as God's Word given for us. It is not merely the culture-bound rantings of a group of Jewish male chauvinists who wrote with ulterior motives within the cultural ghetto of their times. Evangelicals mean that the Bible is inspired because it is God's mind about us, and given to us through human agencies in such a way that it remains true to the things God wanted us to know and respond to.

The evangelical notions of authority and inspiration are not without their difficulties. But we must start off with an agreement that the Bible is much more than the figment of men's imaginations. Biblical inspiration becomes a complex study as we try to understand the modes of inspiration – in other words, how God worked through real people to avoid them contaminating His own thoughts by either their own limitations or the trappings of their culture. This is a part of the very vexed issue of the reliability or infallibility of the Bible.

There remains, too, the thorny subject of inerrancy which has been hotly debated in the United States over the past forty years. It is an important debate but it is also important to bear in mind that even scholars from the International Council on Biblical Inerrancy, such as Kantzer, Boice, Schaeffer and Packer, for whom this has been an important issue, are clear that this should not in and of itself become a test of Christian faith.

It is sobering to bear in mind that we simply do not handle the Bible as we do Shakespeare or Milton's works. We approach with an enquiring humility and with a willingness to learn from each other as we discuss how the Bible relates to science, or critical scholarship.

The Bible is a difficult book not because it is hard to understand but because it is meant to be applied. There is inspiration but then again, there is human perspiration as we seek to apply what we understand. Evangelicals must come to the Bible not with a commitment to exclude others, but primarily to discover its truths as we stand side by side with others who are also committed to taking it seriously.

If evangelical Christians can come to the Bible with this in mind it will provide us with a powerful tool for a cohesive and yet liberating response to the twenty-first century. We will cease to be swept off-course by arguments about whether expository preaching is always more effective than celebratory thematic sermons. But we will hopefully have more room in which to challenge each other about its faithful application to our personal lives and worship settings in ways which seek to be less condemnatory and more encouraging.

The uniqueness of Jesus is not likely to become any easier for biblical Christianity in future years. It is 'the scandal of particularity' which must remain a distinguishing feature of evangelical faith. It is an understanding of Jesus as the only means by which people truly come to know God both personally and intellectually. Apart from this personal knowledge of Jesus, God becomes at best a rational idea rather than a real Parent by whom we are adopted.

This Jesus of evangelical faith is more than a good teacher–philosopher, or an historic first-century guru. He is not only a miracle worker. He is uniquely the 'only begotten' of God. This means that the mystery of the God–

man on the cross cannot be repeated. He died fully to bring humanity fully back to God. No one else was meant to do this. No one else could have done it. Because of this He becomes inseparable from His cross. His life, death and resurrection were real. We are justified by faith in his cross.

None of us is sure how these things could happen. We are no wiser than His mother Mary and when we have preached our best sermon we still ask, 'How can these things be?' His birth, life, death and resurrection taunt and stretch our intellects. We do not stop thinking, but on these deeper matters we 'believe' in order to understand. We have seen what it does to our lives, but we cannot tell how it works and we cannot unravel the mechanics of the mystery; God leaves us guessing and we call them miracles. This is when we know that it is OK not to know.

Evangelicals leave this Jesus intact. We do not reduce Him to the limits of our literary abilities or our broken knowledge of human history. We call Him 'Lord', not because our minds stop searching but because two thousand years have been inadequate. This Jesus has shown us justice and human relationships at their best. He has helped us with our priorities and has shown us how to truly trust by leaving us with the responsibility for the Good News. When they know Him well, evangelicals want to be His disciples.

I did something very naive many years ago. I came across an alcoholic in Kennington Park on my way to church. He was on his way to his Alcoholics Anonymous meeting and, after we chatted for some time, he decided to take me along. I had heard about these meetings and thought it might be a good opening. I was there long enough to get the idea that anyone could contribute. It probably felt reminiscent of our testimony services in church.

I seized an opportunity to talk about how God can change people from the inside. They asked me to sit down. I could be forgiven because I was very young. But I remember leaving the building in the Oval feeling very confused as to why no one was willing to even think about being changed from the inside. In two years of social work training no one said anything about personal transformation either. It was a foreign if not totally unacceptable notion. But every day I met people for whom that appeared to be the greatest need. Behavioural-therapy talks about social policy and its effects on delinquency were all very important but it all seemed to stop short of the more radical prognosis which so many of the people I worked with needed. The Bible calls it being 'born from above'. It is the easiest way to caricature evangelicals, and talk about being 'born again' is a gift to anyone who wants to ridicule the evangelical commitment to personal faith in Christ. It is the ideal way to present evangelical Christianity as a pious holy huddle committed to an other-worldliness: people who withdraw from reality to the privatisation of faith.

But nothing could be further from the truth. Conversion, properly understood, is the most radical religious notion. It deals with the change of lifestyle, character and values of people who have no other explanation but that God radically changed their lives and relationships. It caused a young monk, Martin Luther, to withstand the traditions of a thousand years of church history and say, 'Here I stand, I can do no other!' It forced a young Anglican minister into the open fields to talk about Good News because his heart had been 'strangely warmed'. Methodism under Charles Wesley transformed the Christian Church and probably diverted Britain away from the possibility of a revolution. This personal change has resulted in numerous accounts of very ordinary people who have been prepared to leave home and all that was familiar to them because they have been so radically changed.

True religion simply cannot afford to become entrenched in privatised religion. Credible faith insists on getting involved. Authentic evangelical faith has never been prepared to stand idly by. The very foundations of the Evangelical Alliance were severely shaken at its inaugural meeting in 1846 over the issue of slavery. As an integral part of its formation, the Alliance became deeply involved in international advocacy for religious liberties for Christians and non-Christians throughout the world. True enough, in the early twentieth century it lost the transformational zeal which forced its engagement in relief of the poor and which pressed through reforms for children and factory workers, and played such a vital role in the abolition of slavery in the nineteenth century. 'Evangelicals passed away from the somewhat introspective attitude of personal salvation which it had tended to assume in the eighteenth century to an active benevolence which attempted to demonstrate the Spirit of Christ by helping other people who were in need' (Kathleen Heasman).

Social action has rightly come to be regarded as a part of what it means to be an evangelical, not merely because history has shown this to be the case but because it is an integral part of the biblical mandate. Both Old and New Testaments leave us in no doubt that the care of the poor has always been a central issue for the God of the Bible.

In the quest for identity there is a very legitimate desire to ensure that the term 'evangelical' is used in such a way that it still has some resemblance to the classic use of the word as it would have been understood in the earlier part of the twentieth century. What Oliver Barclay's *Personal Sketch* describes as 'classical evangelicalism' would tend to fit within these parameters. Oliver's book has been helpful in outlining key developments in British evangelicalism over the years, and is particularly useful in opening the curtains on its importance for Anglicans and those who fought to preserve the values of evangelical faith against a liberal Christian assault, particularly in the university setting.

But the evangelical landscape has changed over the past fifty years. Those of us who had the privilege of attending the 1997 World Evangelical Fellowship Conference in Canada will testify to the diversity of the world-wide evangelical movement. The centre of gravity has changed and we now need a definition of evangelicalism in Britain which is consistent with British evangelicalism but which is also true to what God is doing globally. Evangelicalism must remain true to its historic commitment to biblical truth, personal relationship with God and a desire to change society. If evangelical Christianity is about the Bible, it must maintain a commitment to a biblical inclusiveness which admits that the approach to understanding and applying Scripture, developed predominantly by male, European scholars and deeply influenced by a Reformation theology, may still have something to learn from other parts of the body of Christ which hold tenaciously to the same cardinal beliefs.

For example, the Pentecostal movement from the 1930s to the 1950s was very committed to the authority of Scripture. It invariably came out of the context of devotional Bible School settings with a strong commitment to resist liberalism. From an early period the Church of God's official Sunday School literature was called *The Evangel*. Pentecostalism played a formative role in the founding of the National Association of Evangelicals in America and has an increasing profile in national evangelical movements throughout the world.

But in the UK it is not unusual to hear that charismatics have a low regard for Scripture. It is true that there are many examples of Christian groups whose reliance on the Bible is rather meagre. Some of these are newer charismatic groups; others are not. We must remain vigilant, challenging and prodding each other to get the very best from the Bible and to use it responsibly. But not all charismatics are the same and contemporary evangelicalism owes a great deal of serious thought to a growing number of clear thinkers such as David Watson, David Pawson and, more recently, other current contributors such as Graham Cray and Mark Stibbe. All of us have a vested interest in establishing a healthy identity for evangelical faith.

Healthy and biblical evangelicalism need not mean the status quo. In fact, as the Church grows in its range of contacts and cultures throughout the world, a Bible-based definition of 'evangelical' is less likely to be the status quo and is more likely to adjust to the new contributors of modern evangelicalism without losing its historic biblical ancestry. Tom Wright's address to the 1996 Evangelical Anglican Leaders' Conference may be helpful on this point: 'What then does it mean to use Scripture and to do so with that full loyalty which has always been that true mark of evangelicalism? It certainly does not mean ever-decreasing circles of doctrinal definition whose main purpose is to exclude yet more people.'

9

Celebration of Diversity

I first met George Tuck in Birmingham in 1990 when I attended a West Midland Vision prayer breakfast which he had co-ordinated at the Town Hall. George was introduced to me as a 'networker' in the West Midlands who had a very evident passion for church unity, not only in the West Midlands but rather farther afield in the body of Christ. It was still relatively early days for me in my post as the UK Director for the Alliance and I had made it my business to meet with people like George wherever possible. As we came to the end of our time together, George drew my attention to a text from the Bible I had never really noticed before. It was Isaiah 41:19–20.

> I will put in the desert
> the cedar and the acacia, the myrtle and the olive.
> I will set pines in the wasteland,
> the fir and the cypress together,
> So that people may see and know,
> may consider and understand,
> that the hand of the LORD has done this,
> that the Holy One of Israel has created it.

Very nice, I thought, and so what? George explained that although these were all trees, they were very different types of trees. Under ordinary circumstances, they did not belong together and would never be found clustered in the same climate or geographical location. The fact that they could be seen together at the same time and in the same place would need to be a special achievement. Something which 'the hand of the LORD has done'. The text stayed with me for weeks.

It came to me at an important time. It was in those early stages of my work across this range of evangelical groups that I grew increasingly aware of the problems and opportunities facing us as evangelicals. So much, it seemed, depended on whether we could begin to see our differences as a richness. Our unity as evangelicals depended on our ability to applaud our legitimate diversity. To put it another way, we were only likely to stay together if we allowed ourselves the freedom to be different on secondary matters, not merely as a Christian act of tolerance but as a deliberate response of affirmation.

In fact, diversity is far more than just being different. Our differences may lead to passive acceptance that others are unlike ourselves. That can lead to indifference. Diversity implies something altogether different. It is a positive recognition that someone else has qualities (good or bad) which I do not possess. They are somehow different in ways which could actually relate to my being different from them. Diversity is a consciousness about being different. It has a creative deliberateness about it.

The whole universe is one gigantic symphony of 'harmonising differences' from the vast expanse of our galaxies to the individuality of each delicate snowflake. No two items are the same. For years forensic scientists relied on the fact that each of us has our very own unrepeatable set of finger prints. Today, wearing gloves is no guarantee that we will escape detection: where finger prints may fail, our very own personal DNA may still give us away.

Difference is a fundamental fact of life.

But God has left us in no doubt that He is Himself the master of diversity. The God of the Bible does not clone, He creates. And His creation tells us that He is anything but a matchstick maker.

From the very beginning God created trees 'according to their various kinds' (Gen. 1:11, 12). He made living creatures and birds 'according to their kinds' (Gen. 1:21–5). The culmination of God's creative genius was man for whom He created woman so that they might both be aware of their conscious differences (Gen. 1:27).

Throughout, the Bible maintains an important link between individuality and diversity. The fact that we are all designer-made is indeed a part of God's diversity. Individuality may be related to the specific personality of the whole nation of Israel whom God called distinctly as priestly (Exod. 19:6), expressing His personal knowledge and care by calling them by name (Isa. 43:1). It was also shown by God's awareness of the deep and mysterious caverns and creatures of creation (Job 38:31–39:18). At other times God demonstrated His intimate knowledge of people's individual frailty and fortunes (Ps. 139) and their callings (Jer. 1:4, 5).

The nation of Israel itself was typified by its diversity; there were twelve tribes. Abraham, their spiritual father, had been made aware that this nation would be numerous (Gen. 13:16). It is through the life of Abraham's grandson, Jacob, that we begin to see the diversity of the nation with the twelve tribes of Israel. Sadly, this gift of diversity was later to lead to division as the nation lost sight of its priestly role, fell into spiritual anarchy and became a divided nation after the death of Israel's third king, Solomon.

To think of the nation of Israel as an exclusive cultural group is to misrepresent the extent of their deep diversity. What gave the people their national and coherent identity was that sense of purpose; the awareness that they were chosen in spite of themselves to be a model nation for the nations around. Their national consciousness was held intact by this awareness and the fact that the Law of Moses, calculated as it was to erase their slavery-consciousness, gave them a new priestly identity. Even a slave people would have understood the desired transition from a slave mentality to that of a priestly people – even if they could not live up to it. But they were diverse and their laws necessarily made provision for those who lived among them as foreigners. Biblical Israel was not a pure race and one of the greatest Old Testament stories shows that most clearly. Through her tenacity and faithfulness, Ruth the Moabite widow married 'into the family' by her betrothal to Boaz and became great-grandmother to King David (Ruth 4:17) and a great-ancestor of Jesus himself (Luke 3:31).

There was something very different about Jesus when compared with all the other teachers of His day. For one thing He had a way with the people. People gathered wherever He went (Mark 1:37, 2:2). The other distinguishing feature was that He taught differently. They said His teaching was not like the scribes and other religious leaders; it had authority (Mark 1:21, 22), and even though they did not always get the point of the stories He told, usually they could at least understand the story. And then He was different because of the kind of incredible things He did. People were made whole in His presence. They had never seen anything like it before (Mark 2:12).

But there was something else. He wasn't stuck up. He mixed with a wide range of people who were normally outlawed: prostitutes and lepers, tax men and members of the ruling Council, the Sanhedrin. In fact He was always in with the 'out-crowd'. The only people He seemed to stay clear of were the other religious leaders and there was some evidence that He never actually spent any time overnight in Jerusalem if He could help it. He was not a status quo man. He was constantly overturning traditional apple carts and forcing people to think more widely than they would usually want to do.

The problem was that Jesus was working from a rather bigger canvas. He understood God's heart for a greater degree of diversity. His disciples' mission to the 'lost sheep of Israel', avoiding the Samaritans and gentiles (Matt. 10:5), is to be understood as the in-house training before the greater mission into all nations.

Jesus was aware that God's heart for a greater diversity was about to be opened to the world by His death on the cross, and already His ministry contained the seeds of that greater harvest. He already has this in mind with his warnings about persecution (Matt. 10:18) and it became a notable feature of His work. His quiet ministry to the centurion (Matt. 8:5–13) and the Canaanite woman (Matt. 15:21–8) speaks of Jesus' deep understanding of God's intentions for a greater and more diverse family of faith.

Jesus' generosity extended to those who exercised ministry outside His closely knit group of followers. Surprised by a rival exorcist, Jesus' disciples suggest that he be forced to stop (Mark 9:38–41). Jesus' criterion was very basic: if they were with Him in mission they were unlikely to say negative things about Jesus' ministry.

Jesus was uncomfortable, precisely because He was diverse. He did not conform to the accepted traditions and challenged them at every turn. But it was rather more difficult than that. He did not conform to the standard way of handling the texts which they all agreed came from God. Ironically, it was their genuine commitment to the Torah which made them such difficult people to deal with. They stuck to the letter of the Law and missed the spirit of it by a mile. Their limited view meant that they didn't see God coming in Christ. Jesus tried to tell them that the very

Scriptures they were arguing from was the very Word which spoke about Him. Their view of Scripture did not lead them to discern what God might want them to do but led them to prescribe what God must do, when He must do it and through whom He should do it. They never thought that anything could be other than they expected it to be.

That is why they were not prepared for Jesus' cousin, John, and his equally off-the-wall ministry: 'All the people, even the tax collectors, when they heard Jesus' words, acknowledged that God's way was right, because they had been baptised by John. But the Pharisees and experts in the law rejected God's purpose for themselves, because they had not been baptised by John' (Luke 7:29).

It was in the same book, but John's arrival was not a part of their world view. They missed out, not because they did not believe in a forerunner to the Messiah, but because they did not imagine a forerunner like John or a Messiah like Jesus (Luke 7:31–3). It was Paul who expressed the irony succinctly: 'The people of Jerusalem and their leaders did not recognise Jesus, yet in condemning him they fulfilled the words of the prophets that are read every Sabbath' (Acts 13:27).

Jesus' encounter with the woman of Samaria was not just an example in cultural transition (John 4): it was also a major theological jump. The fact that Jews had no dealings with Samaritans was only partially a cultural issue. The deeper issue was that they worshipped differently in different locations. Of course there is no suggestion from the passage that Jesus compromised orthodoxy. He did not condone or endorse idolatry. But He was able to get past a potential theological dead-end by appealing to a greater union of the Spirit and a renewed understanding of truth. Jesus' inclusive approach meant that the woman found herself drawn into a greater truth than might otherwise have been the case. Truth became true to her because she identified its application in her own lifestyle and understood that God was willing to be more generous than the status quo had led her to believe. He shifted her from misplaced adoration, worshipping what she did not know (John 4:22) to true worship of the God of the Jews and the Messiah.

As a result of Jesus' paradigm shift John records one of the most dramatic developments in the New Testament – the conversion of 'many of the Samaritans' (John 4:39) in the village. This not only identifies a major cultural shift, it is the beginning of a consciousness about differences for which no Jew would have been prepared, although God had it in mind all along.

No one should underestimate the challenge which faced the early disciples. If they had the slightest notion what Jesus was talking about in the Great Commission (Matt. 28:16–20) they must have been very troubled. Even if, as some believe, the latter part of the text was a later addition by the early Church, this was a truly enormous undertaking for a group of men who had no real knowledge of the world beyond Palestine. The thought of going to 'all nations' (*ethnoi*) was intimidating, for these were Jewish men for whom a commission to non-Jews would pose a significant threat, as Peter was later to testify (Acts 10:27–9).

That command was the beginning of the course God had long since charted for a diverse community of people whose hearts He would change and who would know Him personally. The commission was repeated again immediately before Jesus' ascension: 'But you will receive power when the Holy Spirit comes on you, and you will be my witnesses in Jerusalem, and in all Judea and Samaria and to the ends of the earth' (Acts 1:8).

This was the golden text for cultural and theological diversity in the young Church. In the first place, Jerusalem was not a comfortable thought. Jesus Himself had spent little time in Jerusalem and, apart from that amazing time when the crowds welcomed Him in procession, it was a place of political intrigue and tensions. More latterly, it had become the place of denial, acute embarrassment and shame. Peter's worst performance ever was linked to Jerusalem. The disciples only had to open their mouths and everyone knew that they were not local men. And with only a few days since that awful Friday, there were still rumours flying around about Jesus' body having been stolen. But the price of a wider Church was that they would start in Jerusalem. Diversity was costly to the early Church and, for the Galilean disciples, their first church-plant in the religious capital of the Jews was not 'home base'.

The kick-start created by the day of Pentecost was very important to the disciples. It helped make sense of what would otherwise have been a totally tiresome task. The rocket-booster effect of Pentecost launched the Church into Judea and Samaria. The record of the Church's presence in Samaria is pivotal.

Acts 8 tells of the important shift from an almost exclusively Jewish Church to the establishing of the Church in Samaria. Acts does not mention the woman of John 4, but she may well have provided a helpful base for the new enterprise. In any event we also meet the Ethiopian diplomat (Acts 8: 26–40) and hear of Philip's itinerant ministry developing.

In the following chapter, Saul of Tarsus makes his appearance. The development of diversity is accelerated through persecution and a dramatic conversion. Peter's arrival at the Italian's home in Acts 10 is about as far afield as Peter had ever been, and for him it had been a major pilgrimage.

Peter in Cornelius' home was not about a culture jump. It was for him a profound lesson in the growing diversity which was exploding all around the apostles. The extent of the difficulties raised by the tidal wave can be seen from the intensity of the discussion which took place in Acts 11 and particularly in Acts 15 with the first major Jerusalem Council. At that meeting the agenda was diversity, diversity, and diversity! The men who had been with Jesus were in uncharted waters. The real challenge for them was to plot a new course between the prejudices of their own cultural comfort zones and the new theology of diversity they found themselves pioneering. The New Testament gives us some clues to ways in which they attempted to sort out the biblical priorities.

Peter's nervous speech in Cornelius' house drew out some helpful points. Given that they already had a presence in Samaria, it is a little surprising that he began by reminding the Italians that Jews did not normally mix with gentiles. That in itself was a surprising thing to say because everyone knew it already. Perhaps he really was very nervous. But he did go on to recognise that God did not show favouritism (Acts 10:34). That which had always been implicit in Jesus' ministry, and which rested at the heart of the Great Commission, had not yet fully dawned on him. This was apparently a new biblical revelation for Peter. The outpouring of the Holy Spirit which came as Peter was still speaking led to two important theological conclusions. First, they too should be baptised. And second, the fact that they too had been given the same Holy Spirit brought them into the same relationship with Jesus (10:47, 48).

This matter of the Holy Spirit was crucial. It was the deciding factor in accepting non-Jews as bona fide members of the new community and carried the day at both councils (Acts 11:15–17; 15:8–12). What was particularly important in the Jerusalem Council meeting was that the elder statesman, James, recognised this to be consistent with the prophets (Acts 15:15). This diversity, they concluded, was not really a biblical novelty. They simply hadn't seen it before. Once they saw it they could not stop talking about it. The Spirit, they learned, seals our adoption, changes our nature (Rom. 8) and brings us into the same gifted body (1 Cor. 12–14) without recourse to the Law (Gal. 3:2).

Now they had to lay aside Jewishness – even a Jewishness which had previously been shaped by the Law – in order to accommodate this new thing God was doing. They decided to allow gentiles to be gentiles with a minimum requirement that they kept away from idols and strangulated meats (Acts 15:28, 29) and they had to remember the poor (Gal 2:10). In reality, these basic requirements were not the end of the story. The theological package grew in the years immediately following, as letters to Jewish and non-Jewish Christians alike spelt out what things were acceptable about the nature of Christ, and the Lord's table, death, resurrection and the fulfilment of the Law in Christ. The letters of the early church leaders developed a theology of diversity which gradually embraced the cultural distinctions, establishing a new humanity in which the cultures and classes of the first century were gathered into Christ (Gal. 3:26–9; Eph. 2:11–22).

Yet there was no suggestion that Jews ceased to be Jews or that people lost their distinctive cultural qualities. Paul still continued to be all things to all people in order to win some of them. That was the skill of the New Testament writings. The same story was told to different audiences in such a way that the cultural marks remain clearly stamped on the work. Matthew's Gospel and the book of Hebrews, to the Jewish mind, and Paul's letter to the Jewish Galatians; John and Luke's appeal to a wider gentile audience and the powerful biblical ethics to Jewish and gentile Christians in Corinth – they all speak the language of diversity in the early Church.

All of them had a very steep learning curve. They had struggled with racial tensions over the treatment of the Greek widows (Acts 6) and the on-going problems of how to treat non-Jewish Christians obviously took Peter some time to work out, with Paul's help (Gal. 2:11). Paul himself, the great new minister to the gentiles, worked hard with compromise. He did not believe in the need for circumcision (Gal. 2:3) but made sure it happened to Timothy (Acts 16:1–3). But there were good indications that this mixture was working well in the Church. In Jerusalem everyone had things in common; Apollos, the eloquent young Alexandrian Jew, was tutored by Aquila and Priscilla in Corinth, and even the runaway slave Onesimus was returned to his master Philemon as a brother. Paul's base in Antioch was also an excellent example of a multi-racial ministry at work in the city.

Paul had no choice. He had to become all things to all people. It was calling more than duty which drove him to it. He, more than any other New Testament writer or apostle, understood the driving passion of God for diversity and, in turn, it drove him. He defended Titus' right not to be circumcised (Gal. 2:3) and yet had Timothy circumcised. He wished himself accursed for the sake of his fellow Jews and even after pledging to abandon them in favour of the gentiles (Acts 18:6) he soon found himself arguing 'vigorously' with them (Acts 18:28) and urging Jews and gentiles to repent (Acts 20:21). The greatest irony of his ministry was arriving in Jerusalem with a positive report of all that God had been doing among the gentiles, only to be told of the problem his ministry was causing among devout Jewish converts who blamed him for the erosion of the Mosaic Laws. In a truly reconciliatory act Paul went to the temple along with others to fulfil the laws of purification only to find himself falsely accused and arrested for taking gentiles to the temple area (Acts 21:20–36). It was his last day of freedom.

Paul's theology of diversity grew out of his own hardships in the cause of that theological distinctive. He bore on his own body the marks of the Lord's diverse body, because it cost him. What Paul had to say about the gift of diversity in Romans 12–14 is worth noting.

Paul's commitment to the body is clear. It is personal sacrifice to God which puts all believers in the place where we become available to God through a change of mind. And it is only at that stage that we can really see ourselves in the right perspective (Rom. 12:3). This is a position of conscious difference; I recognise that I am not the whole but merely a distinctive part of a body which has many parts. The body works best with this kind of consciousness and in this environment, gifts flow so much more easily (12:6–8).

And there must always be love. Love should keep flowing (13:8), it is our ultimate indebtedness. It is needed because we are different. Biblical love is always at its best in difficult circumstances. It gives few merit points for easy love between friends. Biblical love recognises that some are weaker than others (14:1) and that where we may not have weakness we may also differ out of strong convictions (14:5, 6). But the secret is that no one lives for himself. All of us have a responsibility to work for peace, and this may mean keeping some of my strong convictions private rather than parading them in public places (14:22). But no one should actually pretend to agree when he does not (14:22, 23).

Paul repeats the same principles in other passages dealing with the body and gifts. Passages such as 1 Corinthians 3:21–3; 1 Corinthians 12–14 and Ephesians make it abundantly clear that God's idea of diversity is never easy but always desirable.

God began in Genesis with a creativity which expressed itself in diverse variety. He has written it into the laws of nature itself and will finally demonstrate it in that final roll-call of the nations (Rev. 7:9–12). Our community God works best with diversity and has the ability to hold all things together by His powerful Word.

Over the past six years my work with a wide variety of Christians across the evangelical divide has attracted two basic responses. There have been those who have thought us rather reckless in this enterprise for harmonising differences which we call unity. How is such a task possible, and will it not only lead to more meaninglessness as we try to define evangelical unity? They are usually pessimistic about our work. Then there are those who are full of admiration. How do we find the time, skills or the patience to keep evangelical peace, they wonder. And is it really worth it? And how can you work with those with whom you profoundly disagree? My motivation has been to wonder how God does it. How does God hold in one hand an ardent Calvinist who believes that everyone's destiny is unalterably sealed before birth and in the other hand an Armenian who is convinced that we have sufficient influence with God to direct our own destinies through prayer? He loves them both the same and serves them equally. I want to know just how He does that. Dealing with diversity will never be as simple as siding with the ones who are right and arguing with those who are wrong. It is not always easy to know the difference.

Evangelical diversity is worth striving for because our lasting unity will depend on our ability to love and serve each other, not because we are the same in all respects but because we belong to the same Lord.

10

To be a Pilgrim

Before I knew that J.B. Priestley had already said it, I had long regarded truth as a fragile mountain. It stands secure and conspicuous from a great distance and yet it is so easily missed, misunderstood and misrepresented.

As far as the Bible is concerned, Jesus is the very embodiment of truth. As the living Word He is the human expression of God's eternity. This Word, eternal in heaven (Ps. 119:89), was made flesh and lived among us (John 1:14). There is then a pre-time nature about biblical truth which is 'reasonable' and available to human intellect. Truth is not only about ideas: it is relational. It is profoundly about who God is, and how He makes Himself and His thoughts accessible to us. Like a great mountain, biblical truth stretches into the clouds above human comprehension and reaches deep below the waterline of our most meaningful experiences.

The problem is how we encounter this enormous truth, either in its detailed application to everyday situations or, more importantly, how this truth is to be understood in the bigger questions of life and death. That has become the work of theology. Theology is not the same as truth. Our theological footpaths, paved by others before us, become familiar to us as we go back and forth along the mountain. These paths, criss-crossing the mountain, may eventually reach into the clouds themselves, where few thinkers can cope with the rarefied heights and those below may either admire or be confused by those at the top. Some climbers never come back to the plains to help others understand what they see at the top; only a few make the journey back and forth with ease. No one really knows what the top of the mountain looks like and no one believes anyone who claims to have been there. It is always difficult to cross from one path to another and some people start their own path on the way up. Truth becomes even more complicated when you remember that there are foothills all around this mountain.

Church history makes it very clear that even when we have settled the substantial questions of doctrine, we will still struggle to find how the truth is to be applied in some given situations. This means that we are unlikely to do it on our own. We will always be indebted to the insights of those who have been a part of the Church over the centuries before us and we will need the experiences of others who see things we overlook.

As Middleton and Walsh wrote: 'If there is something called truth – as strange as that truth may be – then it is never glimpsed or realised by solitary Cartesian knowers. Truth is sought and found only in community' (*Truth is Stranger than it Used to Be*, SPCK, 1995). Even without the underlying caution about the nature of truth which Middleton and Walsh demonstrate, there is an important lesson about the importance of truth being learned and experienced in the context of community.

Our journey along the Way will be a precarious pilgrimage. Every one of us, with our traditions and theological distinctives, will be forced against each other from time to time as our paths converge, but it is important to recognise and value those who are going in the same direction and compare notes along the way.

When I left my home church to attend London Bible College in 1972 my farewell address probably came as a bit of a surprise to the congregation. I told them that I had no idea what all this would lead to. I had no set plans. I did not consider it as a career move and had no thoughts about the future beyond the course. My decision to study theology was simply the next step. In fact it was the culmination and beginning of different phases of my life.

The amazing and personal encounter I had had with the Holy Spirit was the culmination of years of spiritual hunger. But it did not feel like a conclusion. It was as though a new door had opened into a larger room beyond my own experience of God. It was both exciting and daunting. Bible college was, with hindsight, the start of a new pilgrimage. Since that time, life and ministry have been an object lesson in the fact that you can move your feet without losing your ground.

The greatest difficulty has been to work out what is really true. This has always been a proper concern for those of us with a commitment to the Bible. In fact, the greatest areas of tension for me have had a lot to do with my Pentecostal understanding of truth and how we protect ourselves from those who contaminate or compromise the truth. In this battle for truth it is possible to become guilty by associating with others who believe different things. It is always far easier to enjoy the security of fixed truths we all agree on and affirm in our declarations. Pentecostal prohibition was the way, the truth and our way of life. To leave that kind of secure predictability had an element of reckless danger. It was the equivalent of a voyage beyond my theological horizon. It made others around me very nervous.

I discovered that uncomfortable fact shortly after I returned from LBC and was asked to participate in a panel during a Pentecostal convention. The discussion went on to the Second Coming and events surrounding it. I presented an account of our belief in the pre-millennial Second Coming of Christ. I then went on to talk about other ways of looking at eschatology – the study of the last things – and suggested that we needed to allow some space for the details, about which we could not be too dogmatic. Most people had never heard of any other alternatives. A fellow panellist and senior minister was very disturbed. 'We simply can't be so opened,' he protested. 'We must know what we believe.' He went on to re-emphasise the given position. I understood his unease. I had had no idea that there were any other possibilities until I was obliged to plough through Berkhof's *Systematic Theology* a few months earlier. Options can be confusing.

It was an important marker for me and was probably the very first indicator of how much I had moved over a short period of time. I certainly had no intention of overturning the Pentecostal position or of introducing an alternative one. It just seemed a good idea to remind people that things were not always as straightforward as we might wish them to be and that there were other points of view worthy of discussion. But it was evidently disorientating.

Pentecostalism has been wedded to a pre-millennial view of Christ's return, and anything which resisted or questioned that had the effect of undermining the reality of the Second Coming. It was not something you had to understand but it was something you had to agree with. Imagine my amazement to learn that, in recent years, Elim, one of the largest Pentecostal churches in the UK, no longer regards pre-millennialism as a foundational doctrine.

A pilgrim mindset allows for new possibilities. It may even recognise that doctrine develops to embrace what God is doing in the world today. Early Pentecostalism was marginalised by many sections of the Church as a short-term phenomenon. Campbell Morgan, the elder statesman and Bible teacher, described it as 'the last vomit of Satan' and evangelicals in Germany denounced it as demonic. Pentecostals and later charismatic leaders in the 1970s and 1980s regarded historic churches – particularly the Church of England – as a spent force. On the present showing, both have been proved wrong.

Evangelicalism needs to recover a pilgrim posture: a notion about God and biblical truth which makes us willing to be vulnerable in our security and an attitude which makes us willing to learn from others along the Way who stand outside our own traditions.

As Oliver Barclay's own reflections remind us: 'Diversity around an agreed doctrinal position in essentials is no bad thing. In the end it is doctrine that determines practice, and there are yet fresh applications of biblical truths to be explored' (*Evangelicalism in Britain 1935–1995: A Personal Sketch*, IVP, 1997).

God is just not as tidy as I would like Him to be and the Bible is not systematic. The great Story has many puzzles woven into it. There are parts of it I would not have written and still find difficult to explain to my unsaved friends. How could God, for example, have allowed the deranged Saul to call up the departed spirit of the prophet Samuel by using a witch from a town called Endor (1 Sam. 28:3–19), and why, of all people, did God use a prostitute in Jericho to help Joshua's spies and bring her into the safety of the covenant people (Josh. 6:22–5)? Surely in the whole city there must have been at least one other person slightly more moral than Rahab the harlot? Such questions provide a field day for Bible students, but they add up to an untidy Story. But it is still a great and powerful true Story which we love and to which we commit ourselves. It is always evading us, pulling us beyond ourselves and finally bringing us to the place of awe. For even though there are parts of it which still make us uneasy, we could not write such a great true Story.

Perhaps more than any other character, Abraham's life exhibits the spirit of a pilgrim. One of God's little ironies is the fact that Abraham, the father of many nations, died with only one son born to Sarah and domestic tension on his hands. It is a fact most Sunday School children do not dwell on when they sing about 'Father Abraham'. God works best in our weakness and inadequacies. Abraham rightly carries the main trophy in the roll-call of faith heroes in Hebrews 11. His main claim to fame was that as a man of faith he really understood what it was to be a pilgrim.

What appears to be a very straightforward call and response of faith in Hebrews 11 is rather less confident and characterised by uncertainty and diversion in Genesis 11. The Genesis account gives us the inside story of a young man who began a journey of obedience with his father and was held up at Haran (Gen. 11:31). It was after his father's death that Abraham's call came with clarity and personal conviction (Gen. 12:1). The Genesis account makes it less clear whether his father's original decision to leave their ancestral home in Ur of the Chaldeans was a part of God's direction for Abraham.

But Abraham was clear about two things: God wanted him to go to an unknown destination which He would show him, and He would make him the father of many peoples (Gen. 12:1, 2). Beyond that the details were a little fuzzy. Much of his journey thereafter was an adventure with God in which he was caught up in family disputes with his nephew Lot, adopted Hagar as a surrogate wife, produced Ishmael outside God's plans for himself, and deceived the tribal king, Abimelech. Abraham was not a perfect man, even though he was a faithful man. He was a pilgrim who grew in his calling. God often blessed him on account of his faith and not always because of his faithfulness. Twenty years passed between the original promise and God's fulfilment of that promise. The supreme test of faith in offering up Isaac could not have been easy, but by this time God was not testing a beginner; Abraham had become a seasoned pilgrim. Abraham did not leap into God's purposes, he grew into them. However clearly he understood God's voice in the first instance he had to learn by his mistakes.

That is what usually happens to pilgrims and it has certainly been my own testimony in ministry. For in spite of the many helpful, clear signposts along the way, much of the journey has been a wander through the thick under-growth of unexpected circumstances.

In 1991 I was asked to contribute to a publication describing my own journey into national Christian leader-ship. It was the first time I had ever attempted to retrace my steps and there was a sense in which it felt that life was beginning in my fortieth year. I called my chapter 'Better with Hindsight'. It seemed that I was making sense of many situations in my life for the first time and that I began to understand more clearly what God had been doing over the years. Before that exercise, I had never considered myself as a pilgrim. My chapter gave me the opportunity to gather the apparently disjointed experiences of my life up to that point into something of a coherent whole, and to see God's intentions for me, in spite of myself and the circumstances which had come my way over the years. What amazed me with hindsight was to see that, rather like Job or Abraham during those times when it seemed that God must have forgotten His persistent whisperings about my life, He was still working things out. He had never given up care or control of my life.

As I continue, my recollections also include those untidy bits which still confuse me all these years later. Frankly they have been the times when God did not make sense.

One particular instance comes to mind. One of my greatest steps of faith was never rewarded. It was during my teenage years and at a point of deep searching after God that my local church was having a 'revival'. It was a time in which God met with many people in extraordinary ways. I left the meeting one night fully convinced that I would return the following day to receive the 'baptism of the Spirit'. I believed with my whole mind and heart. I was so confident that I told friends and family members about my firm anticipation – enduring some ridicule along the way! Nothing happened. In fact it was worse than that. There were those who believed less who were blessed more. That was one of the most devastating nights of my entire life. I was distraught because I knew no other way to believe God more.

It was the same bewildering persistence which kept me going when, for years, I suffered from asthma and bronchitis in the pulpit. Few people had any idea just how difficult it was to preach for anything beyond half an hour. There were times from my late twenties to my early forties when I would often abort my sermons because I could not breathe properly. It made no sense to be called to preach if breathing was a major effort. Indeed, I was guaranteed a heavy chest cold within twenty-four hours if I left my home environment. It is no exaggeration to say that this dilemma often distressed me and sometimes drove me to tears. But it was also amazing how suddenly and quietly it stopped. It stopped some time after I accepted the role as EA's UK Director with wider responsibilities throughout the UK.

What made even less sense was the fact that I was unable to stop loving or serving God. It wasn't just an established habit. It was a deeper bitter-sweet relationship of trust in God. It took many years for me to understand that it takes a greater love to love a God you don't understand than to love God as a Delivery Man.

Things did not always add up for Abraham, the man of faith. At the end of the day it was his faith in God rather than the detailed map of the journey which earned him his place among the heroes of faith. Of course, there is a difference between a pilgrimage and general wandering about. Pilgrims have set destinations and fixed points along the way. Abraham was not a hapless wanderer; he had fixed points of reference beyond himself (Heb. 11:10).

I will always remember being present at a quiz night at a teenagers' club during the late 1960s. The local pastor was the quiz-master that evening and he came up with a rather unusual non-biblical question. 'What causes the tide to rise?' he asked.

A club member was certain he knew the answer. 'It has something to do with the moon,' he said. 'And when the moon and the sun pull in the same direction you get a high tide.'

We all laughed him to scorn. What on earth did the sun and moon have to do with the sea and ocean, we all thought. The quiz-master said he was right. And he was.

Sadly, modern Christianity has developed a fixation with the here and now. We have become hypnotised by the immediate demands of the twentieth century and have taken our eyes from those greater realities beyond ourselves. Given our ever-changing values and the limitations of our material world, Christian pilgrims should have a healthy distrust of anything which does not appeal to eternity for its meaning here. In Abraham's case it was God's words of faithful promise which came to him again and again (Gen. 12:1–3; 13:14–17; 15:1–6), together with the fact that God was always pointing him to the future. Our pilgrim status will also depend on our ability to listen well, not just to the appeals of a secular society, but to the enduring principles given to us in Scripture. We have already said that this is not always going to be an easy task, but it must be the compass which guides us along the way.

If we are to grow better than we are, then we must reach for those values of Scripture which stretch us further to the full height of Christ Himself, teaching us what it means to be truly human. The Bible must be seen to be relevant to our human situations. To be Christian is to be human because the Bible reminds us that we are first and foremost people made in His image. He is therefore profoundly concerned about our dignity as beings, made like God Himself, and He watches over our human development from the cradle to the grave. The value of life, human sexuality, attitudes to parents, neighbours, enemies and friends and the consolidation of whole communities and nations fall within the Bible's scope. The Bible is an earth book to help us to heaven, for it will have little value in heaven.

But we must also recover the loss of the final things. It was the key to the early church enterprise. They held everything in the light of eternity. Christian witness, work and ethics only made any real sense because there was the fixed point of final accountability. Eternity is not an escape from reality but the true measurement of reality. It was the reason the great Christian philanthropist and reformer Lord Shaftesbury ended all his letters, 'Even so Lord, Come!'

My own tradition was besotted with heaven and as a child I sometimes felt that there was too much emphasis on the subject. There were some very important reasons for that. In the first place the heavy emphasis on the Second Coming was very important to us as Pentecostals. Underlying our view of the 'imminent return of Christ' (Heb. 10:37, 38) was a dispensationalism which basically measured God's activities in a series of time slots. These dispensations of Law, Grace and the Church meant that we were left only with the final conclusion of all things to look forward to. Jesus' sudden return – the Rapture – would be the final resolution of God's purposes in the world. It was the event which could happen at any time. It was both exciting and frightening.

But it was also easier to look forward to the Rapture if you had very little to look forward to here. Caribbean immigrants in the early years of settlement were a dispossessed people. They came as manual workers to the most depressed areas of post-war Britain. Many became de-skilled, learning new trades and invariably finding themselves at the bottom of the economic pile. Mostly we did not understand the society which we maintained through hard work and sacrificial singleness of mind. Many were abused, harassed, stripped of dignity and marginalised. Early immigrants were strangers in their mother country. It was easy to take heaven seriously, and their focus on a better option came quite naturally.

Most of the songs I sang as a youngster had some notion of heaven woven into them. If I turned up to a church building to find it empty, it was not unreasonable for me to wonder if the Rapture had come! Thoughts about missing the Rapture constantly guided my moral choices. The Rapture was real. This kind of focus on the future wasn't all good; but it wasn't all bad either.

It was not all escapism. It was, in effect, the experience of a vital New Testament theology. Take away the fear which was so often associated with an unbiblical insecurity about our position in Christ, and we were left with a potent biblical motivation for right living. Our ability to anticipate a biblical future helped us evaluate our behaviour in the here and now. We purified ourselves because we had hope (1 John 3:2, 3; Heb. 12:14) and with this hope Black Pentecostals in the days of my childhood constantly encouraged one another (1 Thess. 4:18). We sang about it, believed

it and lived by it. Our church hymnal was replete with
songs which made it seem to be around the corner. We
sang:

> Soon this life will all be over
> And our pilgrimage will end.
> Soon we'll take our heavenly journey,
> Be at home again with friends.
> Heaven's gates are standing opened
> Waiting for our entrance there.
> Some sweet day we're going over
> All its beauties there to share.
>
> Just a little while to stay here,
> Just a little while to wait,
> Just a little while to labour
> In the path that's always straight (and narrow).
> Just a little more of troubles
> In this low and sinful state,
> Then we'll enter heaven's portals,
> Sweeping through the pearly gates.

Strange words against the demanding immediacy of the
twenty-first century, but powerful in their own right. This
future hope was the wellspring from which thousands of
Black Christian pilgrims drew to make sense of their daily
reality in hostile situations. It was not altogether about
escape: it was about survival and power to live. James Cone,
the Black American theologian, helped me to see it better
many years later: 'To a person who would be quick to define
this kind of perspective on liberation as an opiate I would
suggest that the analysis of the black eschatology as a mere
compensation is too superficial . . . It is the divine future
that breaks into their social existence bestowing wholeness
in the present situation of pain and suffering.'

The ability to touch the future so often appears to be the privilege of those who hold most lightly to the present. Most modern Christians tend to have a tight grip on the things which are likely to pass away and have consequently lost our hold on hope. We have exchanged hope for short-term happiness.

Abraham kept his eye on the future and it made him able to finish what he was doing without thinking he had the responsibility for the whole task. By the time he died, he had a number of children apart from Isaac and Ishmael, having remarried after Sarah's death. There is no clear evidence that this father of many nations even saw his grandchildren (Gen. 25:1–11). Like other faith-heroes he saw things afar off, admitting that they were aliens and strangers (Heb. 11:13). True pilgrims are willing to admit that the Story of grace will keep unfolding when we have left the scene. The journey of biblical faith is never completed by any one person or movement in any era. God has determined it so that we will all arrive together. Each movement must do all in its power to read the signposts accurately without the illusion that they have finally arrived.

Which of the original disciples would truly have understood the Great Commission with the level of comprehension which hindsight has given to us? Or which of them clearly understood what Jesus meant when He breathed on them and said, 'Receive the Holy Spirit' (John 20:22)? Paul the late-comer seemed to understand the fundamentals of our faith in ways which Peter could only describe as 'hard to understand' (2 Pet. 3:16) and Tertullian and Augustine gave us a fuller understanding of the Trinity than John.

Change does not come easily to us and there is always the danger of freezing our past and living it out in the present.

For years I had told people in England about my house

in Kingston, Jamaica. I had my own room and we had a large detached house, I said. I also had very clear memories of a huge mango tree and a long path from our front gate to the veranda of our house.

In 1978 Carol and I returned to Jamaica two years after our marriage. It was an important trip for both of us. It was our first return since I left at the age of eight and Carol in her early teens. During our four-week stay I went to visit my father at our old house. For one thing, our meeting was a strange reunion. After eighteen years it was evident that he was still caught up with his own memories of the past and had very little genuine interest in the present or the future. But the real culture shock was the house and the path. It seemed everything had shrunk. I pushed the gate and was almost immediately at the front door. My huge house had been reduced down to a modest size. I had always seen my house through a frozen perception of time as an eight-year-old. It never occurred to me that everything was big because I was small.

We went back to New Town Church and Elder Shaw – the place of my childhood church experiences. It was overwhelmingly nostalgic, still alive and inspirational. But its size was less daunting and it didn't seem quite as youthful. I was really glad to return to this spiritual womb which had given me so much spiritual life in my formative years, but now I felt like a grateful outsider. It was no longer my natural habitat. New Town Church had probably changed, but the greater change was in me and I was ill prepared for it.

If for no other reason, evangelicals need to recover a pilgrim consciousness in order to face the challenge of change facing the Church today. Change is a constant feature of our global village. The best mindset with which to face it is the attitude which recognises that we must always be open for the element of discomfort which comes with the unusual and the unexpected. If the Church is irrelevant, it is not because the Gospel has become outdated; it is because Christians live in the past at the expense of the present. It is always helpful to remember that God is a God of the living, not the dead.

Many years ago I came across a small plaque which said: 'The organisation stuck in a groove will never make records.' It is very difficult to escape the groove. The Church has a vested interest in stability, predictability and history. On the other hand, society clamours for novelty and revels in a culture of constant change. Our senses are constantly stimulated by sights and sounds; a ten-second shot on our television screen has become a boring experience. The two cultures often clash, and many outside the Church will turn their backs on truth because they have confused it with the stodgy predictability of church leaders and outdated structures and programmes.

No one should engage in change for its own sake. The Church is not called to be trendy; it is called to be relevant. The challenge to change has always been a dominant issue for God's people. People who lose their pilgrim culture have a tendency to bed down in the security of predictable patterns and structures. The last words of a dying congregation are likely to be, 'We have always done it this way.' As Martyn Lloyd-Jones suggested, evangelicals believe in 'the principle of discontinuity'. It is the restlessness which refuses to be tied by the status quo. This was the driving compulsion of God's Spirit in the Reformation and other divine initiatives since that time. When we fail to capture this pilgrim mood we signal the beginning of the end in the vitality of what it means to be truly biblical, because the Bible points us to the unfinished future as much as it does to the concluded past. It is as much a futures book as it is a history book.

Our faith in the familiar may cause us to miss what God

is doing in the present. Worse still, we may well find ourselves worshipping at the shrines of our past miracles of success.

This would have been true under Hezekiah's reformation. There was no surprise in his decisions to destroy the idols of the old Canaanite religions. The great shock was his decision to destroy the brazen serpent which Moses made in the wilderness. He had to do it because the people had become so dependant on the past that they worshipped the serpent instead of God (2 Kgs. 18:4). We all have our 'sacred cows'. The problem is that sacred cows are never taken to the altar; they die of old age.

The pilgrim mindset is best suited to face the demands and challenges of the twenty-first century. It is neither reckless, faithless nor rootless. It watches out for the signposts in the Bible and refuses to take the easy options offered by a searching culture steeped in relativism. It will seek to obey, and will not trade off long-term values for short-term pleasures. It wants to understand what God has to say about our world and the people in it: about politics, the environment, family life and our intrinsic value as human beings made in God's image.

But it is not a kill-joy lifestyle. It is prepared to take risks and to venture where it may not be safe. Like Jesus, a pilgrim will talk to anyone about anything and raise the conversation to a higher level of discussion. It is more concerned about the relevance of the Gospel to change lives and communities than about its own reputation. Pilgrims can laugh with sinners without changing sides. In our pilgrim walk we will disagree and object to ungodliness in our society, but we may do it without hate. We may even weep about it, as Jesus wept over Jerusalem.

Most people have become disillusioned, not with the claims of the Gospel but with its ambassadors and institutions. But there is still scope for a Christian witness where institutions exist to adapt themselves to people where they are and as they perceive their own needs. A pilgrim congregation is prepared to reach out for the new wineskins and undo the programmes of the past fifty years in order to become relevant to its present setting. It may mean a different type of Sunday worship or changing the time we meet. It may, as some churches have done, involve a significant reshuffling of our structures to become smaller units of activity in cell groups, or purchasing a pub in which to have user-friendly outreach. It is the Christian Church at its best, taking risks, making mistakes and living for the benefit of its non-members. Pilgrims are unlikely to become dinosaurs.

Wise pilgrims also know that God is on-going: He is always doing something new. They want to know God not only in terms of where He has been but also in relation to where He is going. They will say, 'We have not been this way before.' They follow the wind where it blows without getting lost. And because they are willing to use the new wineskins of possibilities, they are always being surprised by the fermenting unpredictability of the new and creative things God will do.

In 1996 I was a guest at the Swanwick Conference of Christian Brethren. I was pleased to be there because I had made several earlier attempts to attend. I discovered it was to be their last meeting. The council came to a painful decision to discontinue their historic meetings. There was a feeling that the Christian landscape had changed since the meetings began many years earlier and, in any event, the Brethren movement itself was not what it used to be. One of their guest speakers was Dennis Lennon, an Anglican with responsibility for training in evangelism in the Sheffield diocese. In presenting a series of Bible teachings from Isaiah, Dennis drew out some parallels between institutions and movements. He concluded:

'Institutions guard their boundaries; movements are always crossing them.'

11

Firing in the Same Direction

Did you hear the one about the firing squad who gathered in a circle around the victim? It's a humorous if not strange spectacle. But then so much of our Christian behaviour is like that. There is a kind of mutual self-destruct behaviour, which parades as a defence of the truth, so that we often end up inadvertently as Satan's henchmen. More than ever, people with a commitment for truth need to ensure that we are truly fighting on the same side and aiming in the same direction.

The greatest motivation to my joining the African and Caribbean Evangelical Alliance in 1988 was the awareness that God had given me an overwhelming compulsion for reconciliation. It wasn't only my own inner conviction that this was so, but the fact that so many others seemed to confirm this at various points in my life.

I have not always been drawn to the notion. Reconcilers are not glamorous and there is no better way to get injured than to stand between two parties who are throwing punches at each other. What's more, a reconciler, rather like a diplomat, may occasionally appear to have no thoughts or convictions of their own. It often seems to me that politicians are expected to be opinionated and diplomats are appointed to suggest possibilities. I gave up the struggle some years ago and settled into the reconciler's role to which I believe God has called me personally.

We have all been reconciled to God in order that we may have the high calling of reconcilers (2 Cor. 5:11–20). And it is only on the strength of that calling as reconcilers that we have any legitimate rights to challenge others to be reconciled to God and to each other. My work at the centre of British evangelical life over the past eleven years has given me opportunities to see different sides of the same issues; to observe individuals who act as if they are blind-folded, describing the same contentious elephants in very different ways. Or to wander through simple disputes made complicated by our ability to mishear one another. I have also been caught up in very genuine deadlocks precisely because parties understood each other very well indeed.

In essence the ministry of reconciliation has been given to us in order that we might get people to agree with God. In other words, God's purpose seems to be to bring us all back to Himself in such a way that all those who are reconciled to Him will inevitably find themselves in step with each other. That is why reconciliation is worth doing.

My first introduction to the Myers-Briggs Personality Indicator was during Spring Harvest some years ago. The material was introduced in the main teaching to help people understand ways in which different 'types' can complement each other. In May 1998 the Alliance's staff retreat went through a shortened version of their personal assessment scheme. The idea was to encourage self-awareness but it also helped some of us to understand why it was that we complemented others in the work. The one message we all took away from the exercise was that there was nothing intrinsically wrong with being different from others. I left wondering whether we might develop a Myers-Briggs 'church type' assessment.

As we discussed earlier, God the author of creativity is comfortable with diversity. A clearer appreciation of this fact should help us deal with the inevitable tensions and difficulties which must arrive as we grapple honestly with our differences. As Rob Warner reminds us: 'The history of evangelicalism tells us that among those with strong convictions a recurring pattern of debate and disagreement is inevitable.' But it should also make us teachable, able to learn from those who may not be within our own traditions or theological stable. Divisions are likely to occur, not when I am convinced that I am right, but when I become convinced that I could not possibly be wrong.

No one spoke about the diversity of the body of Christ as much as Paul. And he should have known. Born as an elite Jew with Roman citizenship, an intellectual giant and orthodox zealot, he was finally sent out as an apostle to the gentiles, crossing numerous cultural and political frontiers. But Paul more than anyone else also understood what it was like to run into controversy and tensions as a direct result of our differences 'in Christ'.

Much of his writing – particularly Corinthians, Ephesians and Galatians – was devoted to the issue. 'Make every effort to keep the unity' (Eph. 4:3) were not the words of the academic Paul but the experienced pastor who had to do it himself. So he pleaded with Euodia and Syntyche 'to agree with each other in the Lord' (Phil. 4:2). And there was evidently an attitude of humility which went with Paul's boisterous character; having argued with Barnabas about Mark's companionship on their missionary journey, he was later able to appreciate Mark's value to him in ministry (2 Tim. 4:11). Paul's heated theological debate with Peter (Gal. 2:11–14) was not division. It is what happens to family members when they disagree. It is called speaking the truth in love and is needed to highlight a lack of respect or partnership. Whether or not this confrontation was after the important Jerusalem Council (Acts 15), Paul wanted to let Peter know that his attitude was wrong and that his theological lenses were now out of focus. It had no long-term impact on Peter's deep respect for Paul's unique ministry of the Word (2 Pet. 3:15, 16).

The biblical evidence would seem to suggest that if nothing has ever gone wrong in our relationships, something really has gone wrong! Conflict resolution has always been a part of our Christian spirituality. No law book can cover every eventuality, and Christians who look for detailed legislation before they can put things right mislead themselves. Even with the Torah, orthodox Judaism devised 1,521 laws around the commandments and still lost its way. That is why the Bible is concerned about the attitudes with which we enter and leave disputes and has so much to say about humility, self-control, forgiveness and love and reconciliation.

Two significant passages which stand closely together help us with the principles of disputes. Briefly, Matthew 5:23–4 deals with the issue of personal responsibility. The context is of course Jesus' teachings in the beatitudes: it is the new teaching about attitudes to other people. In this instance it is an individual who becomes aware that they have done wrong. In order to make their worship acceptable they take the initiative and seek reconciliation. It is the power of the Spirit's internal injunction which we ignore at the cost of personal peace and healthy relationships.

A day or two after a very difficult debate my phone rang. It was one of Britain's leading Christian figures and Bible teachers. He had rung to apologise for his behaviour. He feared that in the heat of the debate his tone was aggressive and impatient. He recognised as he prayed later that the issue had been very close to his heart and that he had probably lost his objectivity. He hoped that he hadn't made my task more difficult than it was already. I told him that I had not seen his behaviour in the same way as he had. It made a difference to him. He knew where his own heart stood on the subject and he simply had to deal with it. No law could prompt this kind of behaviour. It is the mark of an evangelical clothed with humility.

The accompanying passage is Matthew 18:15–19. My purpose here is not to enter a detailed discussion of this well-used and sometimes controversial passage. There are voices which say that this passage on discipline has to be used with greater caution because the reference to 'church' puts it firmly in a local setting and that it relates to sin, not doctrine. The inference here is that we may use this text where moral or ethical codes are broken. Doctrinal matters, it is argued, may be dealt with more openly and ruthlessly. But the principles remain important. For one thing it tells us clearly that excommunication is appropriate in some situations. It also shows that this drastic step should be the last resort when everything else has failed and not the knee-jerk reaction demanded by so many. The idea is to 'win your brother'.

The passage is an account of the importance of account-ability for wrong-doing and the place for the collective authority of the Church. It is an important point. The Bible makes no allowances for self-appointed autonomous personalities who stand ten feet above contradiction and who know nothing of local accountability to the wider body of Christ. However charismatic, gifted or apparently productive we may regard ourselves to be, the Bible has no place for evangelical supremos who are accountable only to themselves.

In January 1994 Lyndon Bowring, Executive Chairman of CARE, and I jointly chaired a London-wide prayer gathering with colleagues from the London Leaders prayer group. Over a thousand people gathered at Westminster Chapel to pray and worship. Graham Kendrick led us in worship and included a relatively new song he had written. The song included the words, 'Proclaim it on the Spirit's breath – Jesus!'

The words were captured on film from the overhead projector and appeared in a picture used in the following edition of *IDEA*, the Alliance's membership magazine. Within a week I received a letter of complaint. The writer wondered what Graham meant by the words and whether we had checked this out with him before asking him to lead us in worship. She felt that we had been very irresponsible. But she failed to notice the fact that there were over a thousand people who had gathered to pray for the capital and that the evening included a diverse group of Christian women and men from a wide range of churches. She was concerned to protect the truth, but seemed short on grace. Because she got side-tracked she missed the main point.

Jesus came to bring grace and truth (John 1:14–17). He will not have them separated. A lack of grace is ultimately a denial of the truth we claim to defend. Truth without grace may turn out to be a kind of honesty which sets our consciences free and gives us the right to say that we have made ourselves clear, but it betrays the kind of truth which weeps over Jerusalem. Truth and grace is Nathan telling David about his sin with Bathsheba (2 Sam. 12). It is Jesus by a well in Samaria (John 4) or standing alone with a woman taken in adultery (John 8). Truth and grace is compassion without compromise. Evangelicals who write strong letters and feel better for doing it may be technically in the right but still be wrong.

Love is likely to modify truth-telling so that grace is still seen. Love makes all the difference. Where it is missing, we fall into point-scoring enterprises, hurting and abusing one another in the name of Christ. When this happens the lessons of 1 Corinthians 13 become clever sermons rather than actual lifestyles.

The sad truth is that many evangelical conflicts have little to do with matters of doctrine. Invariably they have a great deal to do with our lack of social skills, our angular characteristics and arrogance. If we have love as the Bible describes it we find that we can disagree without becoming disagreeable. Francis Schaeffer's *Mark of A Christian* puts it well: 'What divides and severs true Christian groups and Christians – what leaves bitterness that can last 20, 30 or 40 years – is not the issue of doctrine or belief that caused the differences in the first place. Invariably, it is a lack of love.'

Love finds a way to be strong in our convictions and to put our case for truth without destroying others. Where the language of reconciliation is only a faint whisper the argument may turn out to have very little to do with truth. Augustine's dictum will always be relevant: 'In the essentials, unity; in non-essentials, liberty: but in all things, charity.'

I had read John 17 many times and never seen it. As I passed through the office casually knocking on half-open doors I ran into Mark Sturge, General Secretary of the African and Caribbean Evangelical Alliance. We got into a protracted discussion about unity. He asked me if I had ever thought about the relationship between unity and 'glory'. I hadn't. My thoughts had always centred on unity, truth, grace and relationship with God. But I had never seen unity in that particular light. Mark pointed me to a text I already knew well but hadn't seen properly: 'I have given them the glory that you gave me, that they may be one as we are one' (John 17:22). This unusual collection of men were to be linked together not only in doctrine – important though that was – but also in the presence of His glory. This was surely the theological prelude to Paul's later idea about being 'in Christ', a term Paul used over 164 times in the New Testament.

As I reflected on the idea it drew me back to my meeting in 1996 with Overseer Murray, international leader of the Church of God of Prophecy. It was an important meeting for me, and I found it hard to believe that I was actually in the state office of the leading minister of the movement about which my denomination had so much unease during my earlier days. I knew too that the movement had undergone a significant series of changes which had caused a good deal of unrest as they attempted to be more inclusive. After many decades, Rev. Murray was the first Overseer who was not a part of the historic Tomlinson family who founded the movement in the late nineteenth century. We spoke about reconciliation and unity. He said that it helped him to think of our fellowship as a triangular relationship. Drawing an imaginary triangle in the air, he put Christ at the top angle. 'You are at this bottom end,' he said, indicating the right base of the triangle, 'and I am here.' He pointed to the bottom left. 'As we both come towards Christ at the top we come closer together. Nothing else will do it.'

That is surely the essence of how we must live and work: together 'in Christ'. There is here a Christian existentialism which we cannot deny. We must accept it and work to make it a reality in all that we do in the name of Christ. Our diversity will be held together by the truth of the Gospel we love. As evangelicals, we must be clear about our commitment to this and recognise with sorrow that not everyone will agree with the historic and biblical criteria by which we define truth. But our unity in diversity will also be sustained with grace, tough love and in the presence of His glory.

When Elijah, the prophets of Baal and the people of Israel left the scene, the smouldering pile of stones on the slopes of Mount Carmel were the only indication of the great battle for the heart of the nation which had taken place earlier (1 Kgs. 18:16–40). It was a very difficult time for everyone. Three years of drought had devastated the nation and the sudden reappearance of the mysterious man, Elijah, challenging them to follow God, was more than they could cope with. Their initial response to his challenge was a bemused and bewildered silence (1 Kgs. 18:21). It was a picture of a nation which had lost its way and apparently had no moral fibre left to make an informed and right decision. The national leadership, in Jezebel and her husband King Ahab, was rapidly leading the nation further and further into a post-Yahweh condition. The genuine followers of God were in hiding. In every way, economically, morally and spiritually, Israel was in trouble.

There are so many parallels for us in today's Britain. We have long come to realise that Britain is a post-Christian society. The Judaeo-Christian heritage to which we often appeal remains ingrained in its institutions but in practice our society has long moved away from its practical commitment to biblical values. Britain is like a man with a tattoo on his arm which says, 'I love Jane.' The only problem is that he and Jane separated thirty years earlier, but he has no idea what to do about the tattoo.

Increasingly, our values are being shaped by the consensus morality of the newspaper columnists and television chat show culture. Institutions – including the Church – are slowly losing their influence on the way in which people think or make important decisions about their lives. National disorientation has also set in. Britain now has the highest level of teenage pregnancy in the world and the second-highest rate of divorce in Europe. In 1992 suicide was the third-highest cause of death for young men under twenty-five. By 1995 it had grown to become the second-highest cause of death.

Although there are very exciting signs of life and vitality in many parts of the Christian Church, the overall picture of falling church attendances and the increasing drift towards secularisation tells another story. The indications are that between 1985 and 2010, church attendance will have fallen from 3.5 million to 3 million. Against this backdrop of falling church attendance, the steady growth in alternative spiritualities presents the Christian message with a serious challenge. Many of us were surprised to learn at the launch of Crusaders SOWER project in 1993 that there were an estimated 80,000 Satanists at work in the UK. Today there are well over 120,000 paganists in Britain.

These are not figures for sensationalism and public alarm, but they are clear signals to the Christian community that the days of a privileged position are all but ended. Christianity is now in the competitive market-place of spiritual choices, and one of our greatest difficulties as Christian leaders and followers of Jesus is to face up to the reality of what it means to be in a competitive religious market where all choices have become equally valid. It is the inevitable challenge which faces us in discussing the place of Christian worship in schools or debates on legalising cannabis or lowering the age of consent. We must now compete at every step, recognising that many of our neighbours no longer work from the same ethical code book, even when we happen to come to similar conclusions.

An intelligent Christian community will recognise that the task before us is simply too much for any one part to tackle. Credible Christianity cannot afford the luxury of dividing over secondary issues when there is so much at stake in our society. This, it seems, was something of the spiritual pragmatism behind Jesus' refusal to stop the man who was casting out demons although he did not belong to His own company (Mark 9:38–41).

The pile of stones on the Carmel mountainside were an important recognition of Israel's corporate identity. There were twelve stones, one for each of the tribes in Israel. Israel had a long tradition of setting up altars, but the first time they set up the stones to represent their consciousness as a nation was when they ratified the Covenant under Moses their new leader (Ex. 24:4). It wasn't just that they had a new leader, it was also that they were a new nation coming into their inheritance. For the first time they received a clear and conscious reminder that they were no longer slaves but a nation of diverse tribes held together in a common purpose. Elijah's pile of twelve stones was a very ambitious act. For the last time it also signalled the unity of the different tribes, though it was already outdated as the nation had already divided into two after Solomon's death over fifty years previously, with the ten northern tribes and two in the south.

Elijah's pile of stones would have been understood for what it was: a cry for unity in the face of an opposition calculated to undermine God. Elijah was not on an ego trip. His real problem was that he had such an intensity of purpose that it drove him to anguish. He was zealous for the Lord God Almighty. It has to be admitted that Elijah's battle with evil was dramatic and short-lived. It did not take the nation long to slide back to their old ways. But the message should not be forgotten. The people belonged together, that is the way God meant it to be. Elijah was not dissuaded from this conviction in spite of the political division. In fact, the very beginning of this tribal consciousness was coloured by the tensions in Jacob's family. But this twelve-tribe unity refused to be smothered by its difficult history, and many centuries later James addressed his letter to the twelve tribes of the Jewish diaspora (Jas. 1:1). The same theme is kept alive in the book of Revelation (Rev. 7:4–8).

Evangelicals who take refuge in their own tribal affiliations at the expense of the wider evangelical witness have missed the point. In the face of our contemporary challenges, we need each other. The great tendency of historic evangelicalism has been to pull apart as we grow stronger. It is a natural inclination to invest in our own backyards or to take the easier option, working and worshipping with those with whom we feel more comfortable and who agree with us on most points of our cultural distinctives. This is totally to miss the point. The real issue is the task at hand. Many growing sections of the evangelical and Christian community are now large enough to make an important impression in the local or national newspapers. Our large groups, entrepreneurial skills, growing public relations and even our media expertise may gain us respect or positive attention, but none of us, on our own, is likely to bring serious or lasting change to our world. Our isolated pockets of invaluable activities may lead us to believe that through our relative success and individual achievements we are achieving more than we actually do. It is often our very success apart that can most effectively strike at the heart of our corporate impact: 'Success has meant that [evangelicals have] pulled apart when they needed to pull together' (Derek Tidball).

But the stones belong together. And that's not to be naive. All of us can point to those imaginative and gifted leaders who work better outside the ponderous committees where good ideas die for a lack of attention or faith. They refuse to be 'bogged down' by such meetings and produce more in a year than many meetings will accomplish in a decade. We need such women and men. Not everyone is good at committees. Our working together will sometimes involve committees. At other times it will involve an honest open-handed comparing of notes. In yet other instances, it will include churches working together in local fraternities and interest groups 'for the common good' of the community. In these common activities it should not be beyond the ability of evangelicals to join forces with non-evangelicals, those of other faiths and no faith to act in the common interest of our society on social or political issues. The twenty-first century demands an evangelical Christianity with sufficient confidence in itself to form such liaisons without fear of losing its calling or biblical integrity. If we read the story of the Good Samaritan right, it is hard to do otherwise.

But the unity which is presented to us by the imagery of Elijah's twelve stones has a far more profound message attached to it. It is a recognition that those who belong to a biblical community of faith fulfil God's purposes best when we stand together in order to accomplish what God has called us to be and do.

R.T. Kendall once said, 'Little people defend their own reputation. Big people are concerned about the reputation of the Gospel.' We insist on standing together because of the Gospel. Our unity with integrity is our monument to what only God can do to a disparate and diverse people from different cultures, classes and affiliations who believe and defend the same fundamental truths. And, indeed, what is at stake on our Mount Carmel is the fundamentals.

The Archbishop of Canterbury, Dr Carey, identified a central problem which evangelicals have faced over many years: 'And evangelicals are not good at unity. Since the Reformation, we have been a very fissiparous group of people. We will often be divided over finer points of doctrine until, you know – we think we have salved our own conscience but in fact we are weakening the mission of the Church.'

When we have taken our eyes from the mission of the Church it becomes far easier to major on important minors. Elijah challenged the people who belonged to God and attacked the prophets of Baal. On so many occasions my experience has been that some evangelicals have more to fear from other evangelicals than the devil does. We must learn how to contend for the faith and leave people in one piece.

Some years ago someone sent me a tape of a BBC 5 Live radio interview on which a prominent House Church leader appeared as James Whale's guest. At the best of times James Whale does not present himself as sympathetic to the Christian cause. The discussion, inevitably, was about the role and usefulness of the Church in today's society. A phone call came through from a member of the public. He said he was also an evangelical and proceeded to castigate the House Church leader, accusing him of superficial show-manship and insincerity. It was an amazing episode. James Whale could not believe it and declared himself confused: a fellow evangelical in open disagreement on air when the subject was the relevance of the Church in the UK.

I found it difficult to focus on the rest of the programme. Frankly, even if the House Church leader was a charlatan, I could not see the point of the savage attack on a fellow Christian on a secular programme when the subject in hand bore no relationship to the accusations being hurled across the airwaves and which the caller could not substantiate when he was pushed to do so.

Evangelicals must learn to see that Carmel is a very different place from Mars Hill. In the presence of a watching world we are not in a debating society. We must learn to challenge each other privately and speak publicly with one voice.

Our unity in diversity is therefore to be a unity with purpose. Biblical unity is a means to an end, not a means in itself. It has a mission focus. Jesus wanted us to be one, not to feel good about it but that the world would come to know that God sent Him (John 17:21). It is a primary issue of Scripture because its focus is the salvation of the world rather than the preservation of our cherished positions. This transforming unity is not a cluster of smiling Christians. Neither is it an enforced cloning of our attitudes or beliefs. Christian unity may be sustained in ecumenical settings, but such structures alone cannot create the dynamic of a united body which reproduces the life of Christ.

First, we must see the same things. Writer and speaker Myles Munroe is always anxious to remind Christians that divisions come when our vision is divided. A view which looks out on the world without seeing lost people is unlikely to work well with those who see otherwise. It has always been the peculiar view of evangelicals that the world is more than the product of careless social policy or poor politics. Evangelicals do become involved in social care and political action, but it is never a substitute for the radical transformation which we call conversion. We begin from a basic conviction that human nature is terminally contaminated by a fallen nature. The Bible describes it as sin. We work and serve everyone in society, but we will always be convinced that, outside forgiveness, our best efforts will still fail to produce better people. Educated people simply become smart sinners. Evangelicals will not trade Good News for good deeds.

Evangelicals don't understand everything in the Bible, but they are always trying to and seek to apply it to their situations. An evangelical world view presents Jesus Christ to this fallen world as the only possible hope. In its sensitive and truly Christian expression, it respects all people of faith. An evangelical should seek to protect the rights of all faith groups to practise their faith with freedom from oppression. But an evangelical is also prepared to be ridiculed for claiming that there is something entirely unique about Jesus and His relationship to God. It is to this Jesus that evangelical Christians present themselves as disciples, following His teachings and values as they come to understand its great treasures and challenges for their public and private lives.

We believe that we are saved through faith by Christ's death and resurrection, but we end up working for a better society as a result. We believe that the Church, with all its faults and failings, is important, and we want to remain a part of it because as individuals we also fail and need help from time to time. Evangelicals will try not to dwell on sin, but we are always aware of how imperfect we remain.

But all of that is an incomplete vision. If all of our view is turned inward to the business of definitions and clarification, we have still missed it. We must look beyond our own convictions to see what God is actually calling us to become involved with.

The evangelical situation may be complex but it is not all hopeless. A balanced view of our society brings us back to the tale of two cities. Everywhere around us there are signs that our society is looking for meaning to life. What the late Donald English described as 'the unspoken invitation of our society' is beckoning the Church to respond with credibility and relevance. And indeed, we are in a society where many 'believe without belonging' and where the measure of society's groping after godliness should not necessarily be measured by the number of people who show up for Sunday worship. The latent spirituality which refuses to go away despite the protestations of our secularised, consumerist and technological experiments is the bedrock of our true humanity. As we enter the twenty-first century, 70 per cent of the UK's population still believes in 'God'. Many people in Europe believe in the idea of a soul, as they did twenty years ago. Most people still get married in churches and the vast majority get buried through a Christian church. The very rise of paganism, the occult and the complex New Age phenomenon are easy-to-read signposts to the desire for true meaning.

Even from within the informed corners of our society there are voices which stand in support. In 1997 Demos, the think-tank, suggested that religion should not be marginalised from society or political involvement. Earlier, the Annan Report on the nature of religious broadcasting made it clear that: 'While the churches may be weak, concern about religion is strong . . . we do not belong to a country where all the springs of religious life have dried up . . . A large public still speculates about myth and ritual, death and the meaning of life, holiness and evil.'

The Church has undoubtedly lost ground, but all is not lost. There are still clear indications that where the Good News is presented with clarity, simplicity and relevance, it works. And, usually, in these settings the churches also seek to offer practical help and insights into people's real needs with provisions for community and social care. The 1997 Churches Association of Christians in Local Broadcasting (CACLB) reported a 50 per cent increase in the number of local religious broadcasts. The real need, as opportunities opened up, was for more imaginative broadcasts from Christian presenters.

I was invited to Holland in 1994 to present a series of talks on racism. I was introduced to a young woman who would interpret for me. She had a very good grasp of English and a fluent style. I was commenting on this to my host during the event. She agreed but went on to explain that my translator was a very unusual young woman, fluent in a number of languages, very intelligent, but virtually unemployable. The problem was that she had contracted a very rare disease which attacked the central nervous system in such a way that she was unable to co-ordinate her actions properly. It struck me as a very vivid description of so much of our churches' life.

At the very time in world history when evangelical witness needs to maximise our combined efforts to good effect, we may find ourselves at the point of fragmentation. While historic churches may experience some degree of division over issues such as sexuality, it is unlikely that such an issue will cause any damage to evangelicals in the UK. Indeed, this may help to strengthen evangelical identity across the denominations. The 1996 church survey among EA churches showed that 96 per cent were totally support-ive of traditional views on homosexuality. But evangelicals could drift further apart on issues of faith and practice.

Much of the unease between evangelicals arises out of our attitudes to and use of the Bible. Establishing the difference between primary and secondary matters of truth is still likely to remain a difficult issue. Our under-standing of the doctrine of hell and our understanding of biblical prosperity are likely to present significant difficul-ties for our unity, And, as evangelicals struggle to make our faith relevant to our society, our very understanding of the authority of Scripture will remain problematic. In an age of growing ecumenism, the debate between evangelicals and Catholics will inevitably gather momentum as formal ecumenism becomes a more acceptable, fashionable face of Christian witness in the new millennium of tolerance with the growing impetus of charismatic renewal. This is likely to be an issue which disturbs conservative evangelicals and Pentecostals more keenly than New Churches.

Unfortunately, and despite the growing and steady mutual respect between charismatics and non-charismatic evangelicals, the resident tensions are likely to persist. Attitudes to worship may well change as some sections of evangelicalism incorporate more contemporary forms of worship and reflection into their Sunday worship and others recoil from the repetitive sessions which take up significant sections of the worship experience. As more 'story-telling' emerges, it is likely to provide an excuse for poor prepara-tion and poor-quality preaching. This is likely to be resisted and resented by the steady growth of a more expository approach to preaching which is being quietly reasserted by movements such as the Proclamation Trust and Essential Evangelicals.

Evangelicals are even likely to experience growing tensions on some ethical issues. Not all evangelicals, for example, are fully convinced that lowering the age of consent for gay men is wrong. The debate has centred, not only on Christian ethics, but on matters of equality and civil liberty. The fact that heterosexual, under-age sex for girls is not punishable in law is deemed to be as important as the Christian commitment to sex within marriage.

The ensuing years of our new millennium could yet witness against us, that we have squandered the gifts of diversity and abandoned the purpose of our unity because we have grown impatient with each other. We could, on the other hand, keep our eyes fixed on the purpose for which God has called us at this time. This is the perspective which would get us to bring unity in our diversity.

In this scheme of things we need not belong to the same church to be together. Our togetherness will be shown by the simple things, such as the ways in which we speak about others in their absence. True unity and respect are not measured by flattering statements in public. It's what is said in private which really matters. Unity may also be demonstrated by the way church leaders applaud each other and protect one another's backs, by playing golf with someone from another church or exchanging books which offer a different point of view from our own. Working together means going personally to check out a recent rumour or a newspaper article instead of publishing a cold rebuff on the basis of hearsay. We do these things because we are possessed by a bigger vision: a vision which prompts us to united action should see ever-increasing relationships between our growing list of interests, para-church organisations and the local church. It has been so positive to see some of the antagonism and indifference disappear between the visionary drive of some para-church bodies and the methodical canter of local churches. It happens as para-church groups recognise the strategic importance of the local church and as visionary leadership increases in local settings.

The real challenge before us goes far beyond our ability to fill an ever-increasing number of growing churches. We must refuse to be content. Our task in Britain is not merely to remind our nations of a bygone heritage; such an appeal is only of any real currency when we speak from a common concern for those values. Frankly only Christians continue to use the currency of Christian values embedded in our Judaeo-Christian heritage. People are still spiritually alive, but only nominally Christian.

Evangelicalism needs a movement for change which sweeps across our major streams and organisations, challenging and bringing hope and practical answers to politicians and policy-makers. If we are to have a significant impact on our culture, our impact must be felt well beyond the safety of our churches and important debates. We must set about convincing young people that there is a preferred option to teenage pregnancy; we must find creative ways to sustain imaginative presentations of the Gospel in our schools and higher education. We must persuade politicians that what we have to say about family values, sexuality, justice or health care is worth hearing. If we are to have a serious influence on people's thinking then we must also breach the control towers of the television and radio controllers whose faceless values hold such powerful sway over the multitudes.

None of this can be achieved by any one section of our community. If these things are to happen in our time only a united focus is likely to achieve it. My hope is that this commitment to see change will intensify within the evangelical Church in Britain, that this passion for change will drive us towards closer partnerships in prayer and witness. We urgently need a surge of God's activity in revival that will spill out beyond our churches into our homes and places of work and leisure. This kind of divine involvement is unlikely to come to us through isolated pockets of privatised prayer. Prayer may yet prove itself to be our greatest combined tool for effective change.

Personally, I long for such a vision. A vision like this does not ignore our differences but does seek realistic, open and honest dialogue across our traditions. It will mean very hard work, and some theological deadlocks on secondary issues. But among evangelicals committed to the application of the Bible in our world there will still remain a united concern to see change come to our Church and community. This contemporary evangelical-ism has scant regard for winning internal arguments; it puts much more weight on bearing witness to Christ beyond our church walls.

As we face the demands of this new era, we need an evangelicalism which abandons an unbiblical obsession with the idea of a fault-free Church and directs more attention to accomplishing things for God in the world. When the Church is finally without blemish it will not be by our own efforts.

This kind of evangelical community, of which I wish to be a part, is prepared to be secure without being safe; it is guided and inspired by its past, remains relevant in the present, but is always motivated by future hope. It is an evangelicalism with each of its diverse parts united, firing in the same direction.

In August 1998 Carol and I returned to Jamaica, where we attended a conference. On the Sunday we joined a team collecting church members from the Trenchtown area to bring them to the main meeting in Kingston. Trenchtown – once the home of Bob Marley – is not a tourist attraction. 'Outsiders' do not usually wander round the area, nor through Jones Town, where I was born. But our journey took us through Jones Town and our host insisted on driving me to my old house in Myres Street. As she pulled up outside the front gate I was rather nervous and was tempted to stay in the relative security of the vehicle. But she appeared at my window and beckoned: 'Come on, man!' We followed her into the yard. It was my second visit since leaving at the age of eight. My previous visit had been with Carol in 1978 when I introduced her to my father on the veranda.

This time, as we walked around the yard, I didn't know whether to laugh or cry. I was in the middle of a ghetto. The house was small and semi-derelict but managed to retain a certain pride; the dirt yard around the building was well swept. The young woman and her small daughter who occupied the house with two other families had only just returned from church. They were dressed with the quiet dignity of the poor. She had no idea who had owned the house and had no knowledge of my family. I had nothing to appeal to for continuity except my memories of the place where I was born and had spent the most formative period of my life. Standing in front of the veranda, which I had polished so often in my childhood, I recognised more than ever just how much change had taken place in me. But equally, as I wandered around the cleanly swept yard, I felt I had returned home.

In the same way British evangelicalism has changed dramatically. We come from diverse backgrounds – places where we feel comfortable and at home. Knowing where we have come from is an important part of our identity. We can choose to stay within the confines of those different homelands – sweeping our backyards clean – unaffected by the rest of the world, or we can celebrate our diversity and enjoy our common inheritance.